Shift Your Mood

from Reactive to Mindful

Rik Isensee

SHIFT YOUR MOOD
from Reactive to Mindful

ENDORSEMENTS FOR
SHIFT YOUR MOOD

Rik Isensee has done a masterful job of integrating scientifically-based yet cutting edge material from psychology, brain science, and spirituality into a comprehensive collection of practical tools you can use every day to feel better, happier, and more loving. Rik's sincerity and warm-heartedness make each page glow. This book is a gem.

—Rick Hanson, Ph.D. Wellspring Institute for Neuroscience and Contemplative Wisdom. Co-Author of *Buddha's Brain: The Practical Neuroscience of Happiness, Love, and Wisdom*.

SHIFT YOUR MOOD invites readers straight into the goodness of their own hearts. I particularly enjoyed Rik's playful invitations to experiment with a variety of embodied and mindful exercises. This book will help you navigate the inner pitfalls of your body-mind, as you reclaim the organic vitality of your own life.

—Manuela Mischke Reeds, MA, MFT. Co-director, Hakomi Institute of California. Author of *Eight Keys to Practicing Mindfulness: Practical Strategies for Emotional Health and Well-Being*.

SHIFT YOUR MOOD combines the science of happiness with an awareness of how emotional distress shows up in your body. I recommend this book to anyone who wants to experience a happier life!
—Marci Shimoff, *New York Times* bestselling author of *Happy for No Reason*.

This is an engaging book that contains lots of good advice about becoming happier. Informed by research findings from the new field of positive psychology as well as venerable strategies from mindfulness meditation, SHIFT YOUR MOOD presents a balanced and plausible formula for moving beyond where one is.
—Christopher Peterson, Ph.D. Professor of Psychology, University of Michigan. Author of *A Primer in Positive Psychology*.

SHIFT YOUR MOOD is great—very well thought out, lively, and inspiring; crisp, thorough, and engaging.
—Mariah Fenton Gladis, MSS, QCSW. Founder and Clinical Director, Pennsylvania Gestalt Center. Author of *Tales of a Wounded Healer—Creating Exact Moments of Healing*.

Testimonials

Rik has developed a way to powerfully and immediately change distressing emotions. I worked with his method when I was in the grip of a very negative mood. My thoughts and feelings seemed stuck in resentment and fear. Much to my relief, I experienced a shift out of this negativity to a more peaceful and calm state.

The best news is that I've been able to access this more positive mood in the weeks following my initial success! When negative thoughts and emotions threaten to come rushing back in, it's very empowering to realize I can choose to feel better. Now I have a solid and reliable way to help me shift to a better mood.

—Lori Schwanbeck, MFT, San Francisco

It wasn't long after reading Rik Isensee's practical tips to shift my mood that I tried a couple of his techniques. Sure enough, I was able to adjust my mood during a taxing meeting at work, and then again when I was getting impatient with my kids at home. I mentally put myself in the relaxed state that I feel when I listen to music on a sunny day in the backyard. That grumpy feeling I was so tired of just melted away.

—David Bibus, Seattle

Seething over a conflict, I mounted my bicycle trainer for catharsis. Twenty minutes into my sweat I remembered your suggestions from SHIFT YOUR MOOD. Using the guided assistance from your book, I quickly realized why I was so triggered, then felt calm and astoundingly clear. It was a triumph!

—Alecia Vultaggio, San Diego

As a therapist, I've used the techniques that Rik describes in SHIFT YOUR MOOD with much success. On one such occasion, a client was able to get unstuck from his cyclical pattern of being attracted to his own negative thoughts. He felt a moment of freedom and expansiveness which he could build on. Being able to recognize his involvement in suffer-ing enabled him to break free from this pattern and more fully enjoy his life.

—James Guay, MFT, West Hollywood

CONTENTS

INTRODUCTION

How many times have you felt hijacked by a bad mood, then said or done something you regretted later? Moods can:

- Make *or break* your relationship
- Get you promoted, or *get you fired*
- Help you feel better, or *make you sick—*

Yet once you're able to manage your moods more effectively, you'll maintain your emotional balance even when you're faced with significant challenges. Mindfulness can help you "shift your mood" by calming reactivity, so you can respond to these challenges with a more conscious awareness.

I developed this approach to help you become aware of how moods create tension in your body. You will learn how to *release emotional tension, and shift to the source of your own love and inner wisdom.* Then you'll be more likely to follow through on actions that will help you meet your goals.

SHIFT YOUR MOOD is based on the following discoveries:

- "Bad moods" result in physical tension.
- You can learn how to release this tension, and feel your mood shift.

- Then you'll have a better sense of what you want to do next.

SHIFT YOUR MOOD combines mindfulness and body aware-ness with insights from positive psychology's "neuroscience of happiness." You will discover how to heal from previous wounds and follow through on your best intentions. Instead of feeling controlled by your current mood, you can expand your options: not only about what sort of mood you'd rather be in, but also how you want to live your life.

This has great implications for emotional healing and recovery from compulsive behaviors and obsessions. Yet SHIFT YOUR MOOD is not just about healing; as you gain more emotional balance, you'll begin to thrive in many areas of your life. This process will help you:

- Become less reactive
- Reduce anxiety and stress
- Overcome obsessive thinking
- Tame your inner critic
- Enhance emotional intimacy and nurture your relationships
- Be more engaged and successful with work
- Cultivate mindfulness and deepen spirituality
- Be calmer, wiser, and happier!

Do You Have a Set-Point of Happiness?

Positive psychology and happiness studies have shown that we tend toward a "set-point" of happiness. So whether you win the lottery or lose your job, after a brief period of elation or disappointment, you'll pretty much come back to your base line, or set-point of happiness, within a few days, weeks, or months.

But research has also demonstrated that only fifty percent of our set-point is genetic, so we have a lot of room to raise our basic level of contentment in our lives.

There are a number of actions we can take that have been proven to raise this set-point: meditation, exercise, helping other people, and gratitude, among others. The good news is: *they work!* And even though they are well worth the effort, it can be a real challenge to consistently put them into practice.

Another approach is cognitive therapy, which can help you counter irrational beliefs and change the way you think; but there's often a nagging feeling left over, that undermines the changes you actually want to make.

Why is that? Negative thinking has such a firm grip on many of us simply because it's an incredibly strong habit! We also evolved during a time when it made sense to watch your back and be suspicious of strangers. Whenever something distressing happens, our minds tend to follow the groove of our habitual mental pathways, which often include pessimistic thoughts and negative beliefs.

Getting in touch with our own natural state of contentment can help us relax. Yet this experience of ease often lies just beneath the surface, hidden from plain sight. Having the intention to be more positive can of course be very helpful; but as many of us know, good intentions are often not enough to sustain a substantial change in behavior.

But what if you could *boost your happiness quotient,* and raise your set-point of happiness?

Well actually, you can!

I have developed an amazingly simple but effective method to help you shift your mood and gain immediate access to the source of your own love, wisdom, and happiness.

By shifting your mood, you'll be even more likely to follow through on proven techniques for *enhancing happiness and well-being,* as you live a much happier and more fulfilling life.

Plus, you'll experience immediate benefits:

You'll feel more joy and less stress, as you train your mind to create new pathways in your brain. As you strengthen your ability to shift out of old patterns, you will develop your own pathway to inner happiness.

This shift will help you become aware of how moods express themselves physically. Instead of trying to escape from bad moods by using drugs, alcohol, or compulsive behaviors that often make things worse, you'll become more mindful of what's actually happening in your own body. This prepares you to shift to your own internal resources, which include wisdom, vitality, and aliveness.

This form of active mindfulness is not just another wholesome practice you think you *should* be doing. Once you make this shift, you'll know on a gut-level how you'd rather live in each moment: with a constricted uptight mood, or with *open-hearted joy, contentment, and well-being.*

SHIFT YOUR MOOD can help you realize what you are *not*: your thoughts, the role you play, your stories, or your moods—plus some practical ways to deal with stress at work, arguments with loved ones, getting stuck in traffic, panic attacks, compulsive behavior, or even romantic obsessions.

In the course of this book, you'll meet various people who have put this shift into practice in their own lives:

- Jack felt hassled at work, yet was able to overcome the negative assumptions he had internalized, and learned to assert his needs more effectively.

- Molly's job as a dog-walker was in jeopardy because she couldn't stop checking to make sure she had locked the door when she dropped off her dogs. As she became more mindful of her actions, she was able to feel the internal certainty that she had completed her task, and let it go.

- Nathaniel was constantly criticized by his father, and no matter how successful he was, he felt like an impostor. He was able to counter his own perfectionism and get in touch with his true interests.

- Alice was hung up on a soldier she met in the service, and became obsessed with the belief that his mother was getting in the way of their relationship. She was finally able to register, on a gut level, that he really wasn't available.

- Julio had panic attacks during his calculus and physics exams. Even though he knew his material and had been accepted to graduate school, he was in danger of flunking his best courses. Rather than obsessing about his potential failure, he learned how to relax and shift his attention to the task at hand.

In the beginning, it may take a while to regain your balance when the going gets tough. But as you become more adept at making this shift, you'll increase your ability to soothe yourself in the face of whatever life throws at you.

Breaking free from negative conditioning unleashes the expression of your natural growth. SHIFT YOUR MOOD will help you grasp that "you already are whatever you're seeking," not just intellectually, but through a deeply felt, visceral realization: *You can dwell in awareness itself, steeped in grace and heartfelt wisdom.*

Throughout this book, you'll have numerous opportunities to feel what it's like to shift your mood. Join me now on this remarkable journey toward emotional well-being, conscious awareness, and loving wisdom.

CHAPTER 1

SHIFT YOUR MOOD

FROM EMOTIONAL TENSION TO
YOUR OWN INNER WISDOM

You can't stop the waves, but you can learn to surf!
—Swami Satchidananda

Moods are often experienced as a force of nature that we don't have much control or influence over. They can seem as unpredictable as a sudden squall at sea. If you're lucky, you might see the tempest brewing and hunker down to make it through the worst of it! When you get flooded by waves of emotion, you may not feel much choice about what sort of mood you're in.

While growing up in southern California, my brother Thom and I loved body surfing at Laguna Beach. We could hardly wait till summer, when we'd take off for the coast and swim out to where the waves were breaking. Then we'd whirl our arms like windmills and kick up enough speed to catch a wave just as it crested.

Driven by storms thousands of miles away, a wave is an incredibly powerful force of nature. If you try to resist it, you can get crushed on the beach: banged up, scraped, and bruised. Believe me, we both had our share of tumbles! If we didn't time it just right, we'd get caught by a crashing wave, tossed and churned like tennis balls in a washing machine, then spit out on the sand. But when you align yourself with the speed and force of the wave, you can surf it all the way to shore.

In a similar fashion, waves of emotion can wash over us. But instead of resisting them (or acting them out), we can surf these waves by feeling them in our bodies, and release the tension. As we become more confident in our ability to catch them as they roll along, we're less likely to wipe out when the occasional rogue wave of emotional turbulence threatens to overwhelm us.

People have come up with various strategies to ward off waves of emotion: alcohol, drugs, and escapist behaviors, like eating too much, gambling, sexual conquests, thrill-seeking, shopping sprees, and even working too hard. However, these strategies often lead to more suffering, rather than happiness. By trying to fend off emotional turmoil through addictive and compulsive behaviors, we can embroil ourselves even further in the very trouble we hoped to avoid. Gloating at our cunning dodge of the first wave, we don't even notice the rogue wave looming until it crashes over us.

Emotional strength is not about denying our feelings, or pretending we're not affected by them. *True emotional strength develops from our ability to experience waves of emotion without getting overwhelmed, hurting others, or harming ourselves.*

In my work with various clients, I've developed an easy and active form of mindfulness to help you become aware of how waves of emotional tension surge through your body.

You might not even notice how tense you feel when you get anxious, angry, or frustrated. Urges to act out may even increase as you become more aware of them, but if you don't act on these impulses, they naturally subside. Becoming conscious of this ebb and flow can help you *release the tension, and shift to a more relaxed state.* Then you're more likely to develop a wiser response, rather than react with self-defeating patterns.

Habitual Pathways

Neurons that fire together, wire together.

—Donald Hebb

Feelings are expressed through our bodies. By bringing our awareness to physical sensations, we become more mindful of emotional states and core beliefs that continue to shape and influence our current experience. I believe these core beliefs (even if they're delusional!) serve a protective function. Bringing a mindful awareness to this protection can gently challenge previous assumptions, and stimulate a shift toward healing.

These beliefs create *neural pathways* that are reinforced by similar experiences over time. I like to think of neural patterns as "grooves" in the brain: any event that resembles a previous experience tends to slide right into that groove, eliciting a familiar feeling. Before we know it, we're sucked into the vortex of our previous conditioning, reactivating these habitual pathways, which leads to a similar emotional reaction.

The fields of cognitive therapy and positive psychology have demonstrated that challenging our assumptions and developing our strengths can expand our options for healing and growth, by creating new attitudes and behaviors that enhance happiness and well-being. In addition, neurologists have discovered that the brain is capable of far more change than we previously thought. This *neuroplasticity*—the ability of neurons to create new pathways—suggests that our emotional reactions are not limited to previous patterns, so we can expand our range of responses.

Getting in touch with how moods manifest in your body can help you choose how you want to focus your attention: trapped in the habitual pathways of your past, or opening to the spaciousness of the present moment? Over time, you'll increase your ability to shift out of the vortex of your usual pattern to a much more relaxed and wiser resource, which is *already within you.*

Your Guard Dog

Reactivity grows out of your need to protect yourself. So when something reminds you of a familiar danger, your automatic reactions may get stimulated, triggering a cascade of associations and responses that are intended to protect you. This is what our conditioning is all about: guarding us from danger to our self-image, self-esteem, and even our personal safety.

You can think of this familiar reaction, or strategy, as your *Guard Dog*. Your guard dog is not an enemy; it arose to keep you safe. The problem is that your guard dog's strategies may have developed when you lacked the resources to come up with anything else. So your guard dog may have a limited number of tricks to respond with, some of which can be pretty self-defeating!

But luckily, in addition to our guard dog, we also have an inherent knowledge of what's really right for us: how we deserve to be treated, our true interests, and what we aspire to. Even in the face of difficult times, we can get in touch with our own internal wisdom. But it's fairly subtle, so we need to pay attention to it in order to develop it as a viable alternative to our usual reactions.

We're often not even aware of how physically uptight we are. All we know is that we're feeling uncomfortable, antsy, out of sorts, or irritable. And we're naturally drawn to substances or activities that give us some temporary relief. But after the drug wears off, we've stuffed ourselves, or we've spent or gambled away all our money, those same annoying feelings come back—with a vengeance!—since now we're hung over, bloated, or broke.

A mindful awareness of our physical reactions enables us to develop that part of ourselves that notices what's coming up in any given moment. By becoming aware of physical sensations, we have a better chance of working through our emotions, rather than getting hooked into our familiar reactions, or acting out in some unconscious way.

So let's see if we can develop a more realistic approach to managing our moods without over-reacting, acting out, or otherwise getting stuck in unproductive patterns; and instead, shift to the source of our own loving attention and inner wisdom.

How to Shift Your Mood

First we'll develop a mindful state, and get in touch with a familiar place that feels nurturing, comforting, and safe. From that relaxed place of comfort and ease, we'll explore that part of yourself that feels vulnerable, agitated, or con-stricted. Then we'll look at where you feel that tension in your body. I will offer some suggestions for deepening your awareness, then we'll try a couple of experiments. Give yourself enough time for these suggestions to sink in, before moving on to the next phase. You can also pause and close your eyes to help you get in touch with your experience.

Take in a deep breath, and let it go. Take in another breath and this time hold it for a moment, then let it go. Relax into your seat, supported by your cushion. Experience the pull of gravity and the framework of your bones and muscles holding you up. Feel the sensations of your breath, even your heart beating—life is pulsing through you.

Allow yourself to arrive in a mindful place, simply aware of your own experience as you settle in and adjust. You may feel curious, apprehensive, or even skeptical. That's fine; every reaction is welcome here. I'd like to suggest approach-ing this moment with loving kindness, curiosity, and a com-passionate attention for whatever arises.

Imagine a place that seems very familiar, where you feel warm, comfortable, welcome, and safe. It may be outdoors, by a lake, at the seashore, in the mountains, or at a park, where you can smell the fresh air. Or it may be some cozy place inside, on the couch, or in a favorite chair by the window.

A number of possible places may come to mind, so just go with one that you're drawn to and allow yourself to rest there, noting the various sensations you're aware of around you—sights, sounds, coolness of the breeze, any familiar smells—and allow yourself to relax into comfort, safety, and rest. This home base is a wonderful resource that you can always come back to.

From this more relaxed place, we're now going to shift your attention toward an issue you'd like to get a better handle on in your life.

Give yourself some time to make this transition, and see how your body responds as you get in touch with a tender part of yourself that feels agitated or vulnerable. Maybe you've felt hurt, neglected, or mistreated in some way; you're troubled by some looming decision; or you're aware that you're judging yourself.

Feel this reaction in your body: you may sense it as a form of constriction, pulling back, or pushing away. Take your time, and just see if you can get in touch with it. If you don't really feel anything, that's all right; we're just exploring what might be happening internally in response to this emotional vulnerability.

If you're aware of a physical reaction, just stay with that sensation and pay attention to the quality of this clenching, tightness, or constriction, however you experience it: where it's located in your body, how big it is, whether it's cool or warm, soft or hard, how deep inside it feels, whether it seems to be moving or growing; whatever form it takes. Take a few moments to really investigate how these sensations manifest right now, in your body.

Now notice any associations you may have with this vulnerable feeling: perhaps a memory, an image, a sound, or a smell—other thoughts, emotions, or beliefs—and any conclusions you may have come to in response to earlier events or circumstances. You don't have to go searching for them, just observe any associations that naturally occur to you.

Notice any impulses—wanting to pull away, or flee—or any feelings that arise, like a hint of tears behind your eyes. Just pay attention to whatever occurs to you, welcoming and allowing whatever you're aware of. See what begins to happen after a while—any shift in your experience—and allow whatever else wants to emerge.

Now I'd like to suggest a phrase to try on, just to see if it resonates. If it sinks in, welcome that feeling and enjoy that sense of recognition. If you're skeptical, not sure, if you find yourself rejecting it, that's fine; just be aware of whatever comes up for you.

Go inside for a moment and feel what happens in your body when you read this phrase: *You're all right, just the way you are.* Try saying it again out loud, and see if anything shifts, physically.

Keep breathing, and feel how these words land in your body: if they allow you to relax, or if you find yourself rejecting this idea with some tension. Maybe it brings up some thoughts, a memory, or maybe nothing at all. If you're able to let this phrase in, feel what shifts in your body, and savor that experience of well-being.

If you find yourself rejecting it, coming up with objections, welcome those objections; they are important clues. Perhaps you've reached some conclusions or developed some core beliefs that reject this thought. Where do you feel this reaction in your body? Hold onto it as long as you wish, and discover what wants to happen next.

Again, this tension is not your enemy. It's like the guard dog we spoke about earlier, which arose out of a need you felt somewhere along the line to protect yourself. Your guard dog may be activated, scanning the environment with hyper-awareness!

Instead of trying to escape from it, allow yourself to feel this tension and constriction. Even crank it up a notch, just so you can experience the full force of this activation in your body. Your body already knows how to make this constriction feel more intense.

And now ease off. Your body also knows how to relax this tension. Take your time to register each part of your body that's mobilized both to increase this tension, and to relax it.

Now crank it up again, increasing the constriction. Crank it up even more, to a second notch so it's pretty tight (don't strain yourself, just tight enough to really register the constriction). Take in a deep breath and hold it for a moment, while maintaining this tension.

Hold it—hold it—hold it—then release your breath, let go of the tension, and let your breathing return to normal.

Pay attention to whatever you're experiencing right now, physically. Probably some relaxation, even some relief. You may find that it's fairly pleasurable to feel relaxed, especially after holding your body with such tension. Allow yourself to savor that relief and ease into it. If you wish, you can even go back to that lovely place of warmth, comfort, and safety we started out with.

As you're resting, check in with yourself to see if you prefer being in this more relaxed state, rather than the tension you were previously feeling. This natural preference is a wonderful resource, as you become acutely aware that you have a choice between constriction and relaxation.

It's probably not all that difficult for most of us to decide; it's like asking yourself whether you really want to keep banging your toe, or clunking yourself in the head! And yet I've also worked with some people who felt a certain power (or self-protection) in the constriction as well, and they're not so eager to give it up. If that's true for you, then simply allow yourself to feel the strength of that self-protection.

Whatever your experience was, you can gently remind yourself, as soon as you notice that you're caught in a tense reaction, to become aware of your physical experience; then crank it up, and let it go.

From this more relaxed place, I suspect you also have a helpful perspective about the previous pattern. So stay inside, and get in touch with your own internal wisdom: what could you tell that part of yourself that gets cranked up with the tension you were feeling just a moment ago? What do you know now, from this wiser resource, that could reassure your guard dog?

If words are accessible to you, try coming up with a whole sentence: maybe something along the lines of "I can deal with this," or "I don't need to get caught up in this drama," or "I can prepare myself," or even "I really am all right just the way I am."

Now we're coming to the close of our experiment. Bring a mindful awareness to your experience of this journey, and take in another deep breath. Gradually become aware of your body on your cushion and other sounds in the room; slowly move your fingers, feel your breath and other sensations inside your body, grounding yourself in the present moment. When you're ready, take a moment to look around, and take in the rest of the room.

Assuming this process worked, you just got in touch with the source of your own internal wisdom, even in the face of your usual constriction. You also have a real sense, on a gut level, of your actual preference. It's not just an idea; it's a felt experience.

This physical shift and momentary insight may not entirely address the content of the thoughts, concerns, or worries that made you uptight in the first place. Even if you have an idea of what you'd like to do next, you may not have the confidence to follow through. Or you may still have a problem you need to deal with, and you're not sure how, but you can come to it from a more relaxed perspective, tapping into the resource of your own wisdom.

You can always return to this source of wisdom—it's like a deep well you can dip into any time you want. It's always right here, right now. All you have to do is take in a deep breath, and let it go.

If this experiment didn't work for you, it may be that you've shifted to a more guarded position, which is fine! There could still be a need to protect yourself, and it's important to honor the fact that you were resourceful enough to call in your guard dog to keep you out of harm's way.

Take a moment, and just allow yourself to experience the power of that self-protection. Feel how that strength shows up in your body. Give your guard dog a voice: it may be something like "Don't mess with me!" or "Leave me alone." Then see what it's like to simply respect that voice, and see if anything shifts.

Practice going back and forth between contraction and release. Just see what comes up for you, and discover your true preference. What does this powerful part of you know about your current situation?

It may take some time and further validation before your guard dog feels reassured enough to release the tension that you often feel. (Take a look at the section called "Seven Steps to Calm Your Guard Dog and Tame Your Inner Critic" in chapter 6 for some helpful strategies.) Over time, you'll increasingly be able to soothe your guard dog as you shift your mood.

In the beginning, it may take a while to catch yourself; but as you get more practice, this process will come more naturally to you, and feel a lot more accessible.

FIRE Wisdom

Here's a brief summary of how to shift your mood, which I call **FIRE** wisdom! The acronym **FIRE** provides a handy way to remember these steps; plus it's helpful to realize your own internal wisdom is available, just under the surface, even when you get fired up! Just like real fire can be both dangerous and beneficial, **FIRE** wisdom can help you manage your moods more effectively. Whenever you're feeling agitated or uptight, try these four steps to shift your mood:

1. **Feel** how the emotional tension shows up in your body.
2. **Intensify** the physical sensation, and hold your breath for a moment.
3. **Release** the tension
4. **Explore** your preference: whether you'd rather feel uptight, or relaxed?

And now, become aware of your own internal wisdom:
What do you know now, from this more relaxed place, about whatever was bothering you? How would you like to handle whatever situation you are faced with?

CHAPTER 2

YOU ARE NOT WHAT YOU THINK

NOT YOUR THOUGHTS, YOUR ROLE, OR YOUR STORY

Whatever you dwell upon—that will become the inclination of your mind.

—Buddha

It can be helpful to look at some of the ways we get emotionally hijacked in the first place. Some of the main culprits include:

1. Faulty thinking
2. Being overly identified with the roles we play in life, and
3. Confusing who we are with the stories we tell ourselves.

This chapter will provide a number of experiences to help you get in touch with your own internal awareness. We'll explore what's going on inside our minds besides thinking, the roles we play, and the stories we tell ourselves.

You Are Not What You Think

"You are not what you think" in two senses:

1. You are not just your thoughts; and
2. You are not who you think you are.

It's easy to assume that we are the sum total of all our thoughts, yet we are not just our thoughts. There's a whole world of internal experience aside from what we are thinking—sights, sounds, smells, tastes, and physical sensations—plus an awareness of ourselves, our being-in-the-world, that's not dependent on thought.

Try this:

Go inside for a moment, and bring your attention to various sensations: what can you hear right now? Feel the pressure on your back and legs from sitting. Now bring your attention to your hands, sensations of warmth or coolness. Are you aware of any tastes or smells? Look around and see what's in your field of vision. Wiggle your toes. Now bring your awareness to your breath. Take in a nice big breath, and let it go.

This simple moment of physical awareness helps you realize that you are not just your thoughts. This recognition registers in our bodies, as well as our minds.

Every organism has a natural ability to regulate itself. There is so much our body automatically takes care of: our heartbeat, blood pressure, digestion, and immune system; healing cuts, strains, and bruises; even our breathing is fairly automatic. And our body sends us signals when we need to take care of it, as well: we feel cold, hungry, thirsty, or tired; so we put on a sweater, eat, drink, and rest. Even with emotional needs, we're often aware of our feelings through bodily sensations: we feel the ache of loneliness, and reach out for companionship.

That may seem fine for physical and even emotional needs, but what about all the rest of our responsibilities? Don't we have to think through everything else we need to do?

Of course it makes sense to plan whatever tasks you need to accomplish. But aside from that, we probably spend a lot of time rehearsing and obsessing about details that don't matter a great deal, or that will take care of themselves once we're involved in the situation itself. We don't need to plan everything out, spin our wheels, or work that hard! While it makes sense to plan for our future and be adequately prepared for any job we undertake, we can also trust in the natural unfolding of our own responsiveness.

Try this:

Go inside again, and just allow yourself to get in touch with your bodily sensations. Shift your weight to get more comfortable. Notice if you're thirsty, hungry, sleepy, or if you need to use the bathroom.

This may seem like a very mundane example, but when left to themselves, our bodies have a self-regulating wisdom that knows exactly what we need at any given moment. By becoming more aware of our actual physical needs, we're less likely to overeat, drink too much, or have sex when we don't really feel like it.

So we are more than just our thoughts. Yet thoughts are not a problem; they can be useful tools that help us deal with various interests and concerns. Thinking can help us mediate between impulse and harsh judgment. It can actually help us make more conscious choices about where we'd rather locate ourselves: in our previous conditioning, or in the open-hearted awareness of the present moment? We're more likely to cultivate that soothing awareness when we bring a gentle mindfulness to whatever arises.

So what's the problem? It's becoming over-identified with our thoughts, or mindlessly acting out our conditioning, that gets us into trouble. Instead, just bring a gentle awareness to your physical sensations, responsiveness, and natural unfolding.

You Are Not the Role You Play

We are not just our thoughts, but we are also more than who we think we are in terms of the roles we play.

We often find ourselves immersed in various identities: as a woman, a man, a citizen of a nation; from a certain ethnic background, religion, or sexual orientation; with various roles as son, daughter, parent, or spouse; perhaps identified with a particular profession, or with our own personality and history.

Since our culture has a way of defining us according to our roles, we may associate our self-worth with what we can accomplish. We absorb many of these expectations from our parents, school, friends, media, religion, and the surrounding culture. And we may come up with some expectations for ourselves, according to our own interests and values, or even what we want to accomplish during our lives. Many of these ideas can be very productive, express our natural talents, and even contribute to the world around us. But these identities can sometimes get in the way of experiencing who we actually are—beyond our various roles—in the present moment.

The Impostor

I had a client named Nathaniel, whose family emigrated from China. (In all the examples throughout this book, names and some details have been changed to protect confidentiality.)

As the eldest son of three children, he felt a keen responsibility to be successful. His father was a small businessman who was acutely conscious of being an Asian immigrant in a mostly Caucasian community, and he wanted his children to reflect well upon the family and his local business. He sold cut flowers to the burgeoning hospitality industry in the resort town where they settled. Nathaniel's mother was very loving, but also took her role quite seriously, and taught her children how to behave properly in every kind of social situation. She called this obligation _zhòng hè_ (which literally means "heavy burden"): they must always perform at their best, and never bring shame upon the family.

So Nathaniel rose to the challenge and became very successful in his own right (as did both his siblings). He got an MBA and became vice president of the local bank. He joined the boards of various non-profits. He was an excellent speaker, and was frequently asked to attend official functions and fund-raisers.

But despite his success (and despite the fact that he frequently treated his father to vacations abroad after his mother died), his father constantly criticized him. It seemed as though, in his father's eyes, he couldn't do anything right. Whether it was the home he bought, the friends he chose, how he dressed, or even the trips he planned, nothing was good enough: "Why are you just vice-president of the bank? Why couldn't you be president? If you're so smart, why didn't you become an engineer, like your brother? You got your MBA, why settle for being an employee? Start your own business, like I did!"

Over time, Nathaniel developed what he called various "holograms," which meant a kind of mask, persona, or role he played in the world around him. These included the dutiful son, the vice president, and the corporate speaker. He was quite successful at all of these, but they left him feeling like a phony or an impostor. He assumed that if anyone knew the real Nathaniel, they wouldn't like him. Even though he could function well at work-related functions, there were times when all he really wanted to do was sit at home and not be bothered by any responsibilities.

In some ways, Nathaniel can be seen as an example of the "model minority" status of Chinese immigrants in the United States. They are expected to do well, which sometimes creates an incredible pressure to perform. And as the first son of a demanding father, he was very successful. But it left him feeling empty.

So I asked him to go inside to explore this dilemma: if there was some way he could live his life more authentically, from within, not gauging his self-worth by his various roles, or by the unrealistic demands of his father.

When he closed his eyes, his immediate image was that he was struggling to get out of a deep well. After climbing the walls and sliding back down every time, he got discouraged.

I said "Feel how this struggle shows up in your body." He felt very tense, and frustrated by the struggle. Then I asked, "What would it be like to give up the struggle, and just sink to the bottom?"

"Ooh, it's all yucky, full of slime and goo." After his initial repulsion, however, he relaxed considerably into the muck at the bottom of the well. "I don't have to do anything here. Nobody expects anything of me, 'cause after all I'm stuck in the bottom of a well."

So we let him relax for a while, not having to do anything or be anybody. After a few minutes, though, he got bored. "Is this all I'm supposed to do? Just sit at the bottom of a well and do nothing?"

I asked, "What else would you like to do?"

"If I throw a rope over the crank, I guess I could haul myself up in the bucket."

"It's really up to you," I said, not wanting him to perform just for my sake.

Over a period of several months, Nathaniel gradually got in touch with his own internal wisdom about how he wanted to live a more authentic life. He went back and forth between being out in the world, and retreating to his home. Whenever he felt uptight, he took that as a signal that he was performing for others, rather than himself. Then he'd crank up the tension, hold his breath, and let it go.

He quit one of the boards he had joined simply to make a good impression. Then he volunteered as a tutor at a local school, which he found very fulfilling. He went back to making ceramics, a hobby he had always enjoyed, but never thought he could justify the time. He enjoyed just spinning the potter's wheel as he formed a vessel of clay; he said it was very "centering" for him!

He made some pots for his friends, which he fired at a local kiln. He got more in touch with what it was like just to be himself and follow his own interests, rather than anticipating how he was supposed to perform.

As he became less perfectionistic toward himself, he also became less demanding of others. Having grown up with a close connection to the hospitality industry (he delivered his father's flowers when he was a teenager), he used to be highly insulted if he felt mistreated at a four-star hotel. He'd write a letter of reprimand to get the employee fired. Now he was able to take mishaps less personally, and feel less aggrieved. He was also less concerned about his image. Even though he loved his Prada shoes, he often wore cheap sandals whenever he wasn't at the bank or some charity gala.

His father, remarkably enough, was even overheard bragging about what a great son he was at an event where Nathaniel gave a well-received speech that was written up in the local Chinese-language newspaper. It was still a sore point for Nathaniel that his father would never express his approval directly. He even told him so, which in the past he never would have dared. His father blustered about, and said he didn't want to give him a big head, but that he was proud of him, and grateful for all he had done for him since Nathaniel's mother died.

Role Diffusion

If we define ourselves solely in terms of our outward accomplishments, we can become very disoriented when major life-changes occur. Getting laid off, divorced, having an accident, or a major illness can be a significant loss. But even the natural outgrowth of all you have worked for—the kids leave home, or you finally retire—can also bring about a major shift in your usual role. Some people jump to nega-tive conclusions in response to this shift in roles: I'm not a good partner, breadwinner, parent; or there's no use for me anymore.

Role diffusion is the term often used to describe this diso-rientation, and after the loss of a significant role, it can be helpful to discover other ways to contribute to the world.

But I'd like to challenge the assumption underlying the link between self-esteem and fulfilling a particular role: we don't have to over-identify with *any* of the roles we play as carpenter, parent, lawyer, teacher, or spouse. As important as any of these roles might be to us, they are not the sum total of who we are. We are simply beings in the world, and by our very nature we can naturally unfold in an organic way, responsive to our environment.

Try this:

Go inside for a moment, take a deep breath, and let it go. Allow yourself to discover your own awareness: what's really there, without all your usual assumptions? Does this aware-ness have an identity as male or female, young or old, with a particular ethnicity or religion, rank, or profession? Or can there just be an open-hearted awareness, aside from any of the roles you play?

Many people fear they will melt into complacency if they don't hold a whip over themselves. Nathaniel, for example, was afraid he'd get lazy and just loaf around watching soap operas, eating bon-bons. Yet once he released himself from his perfectionism, he re-discovered his previous interest in ceramics. So what if he wasn't as "productive" as he used to be? Tutoring kids at the neighborhood school even led him to consider whether he'd like to adopt a child with his partner.

So how do we find out who we are, aside from our thoughts, and aside from the various roles we play? Mindfulness offers an exquisitely fine-tuned way to discover ourselves, from moment to moment, outside of our usual preconceptions.

Try this:

Go inside for a moment, and take a deep breath, then let it go. Just try being quiet for a moment, with nothing to do, nowhere to go, and nothing to accomplish.

What it's like *being*, rather than *doing*?

Feel what happens in your body when you read this phrase: *You don't have to justify your existence.*

You Are Not Your Story

No story, no self (no problem!)

Instead of falling prey to a chain reaction of revenge or self-hatred, we gradually learn to catch the emotional reaction and drop the story lines.

—Pema Chödrön

We're not just our thoughts or the roles we play, and we're not simply the sum of all the stories we tell ourselves. If we stop telling ourselves so many stories about who we think we are, even for a moment, we discover another way of *being*.

Of course, there's nothing wrong with family history, amusing anecdotes, and taking joy in various accomplishments.

And it's gratifying to share our memories, feel heard, and be acknowledged. Telling stories is how we create and enrich our world! Nonetheless, there's also a danger of getting stuck in who we think we are, and limited by the stories we tell ourselves.

Knowing that we're not just our story can help us counter all the judgments, obsessions, justifications, and *angst* that keep our anxiety going. Then we're less tempted to escape through various distractions: alcohol, drugs, compulsive eating or sex, and other self-defeating behaviors.

If you're not your story, then who are you? Some meditation traditions suggest there's no real ongoing "self" you can grasp on to. This idea can be somewhat puzzling for westerners. We're very much imbued with the importance of the individual, self-esteem, and having a firm sense of who we are.

It's not as though you don't exist—you obviously do! But the supposition that there's some consistent and solid self-identity can be misleading. When we're overly invested in a self that we've defined in a particular way, sooner or later that "self" begins to shift: whether through illness, loss, aging, or our own natural development. Our story (or our self-image) no longer matches reality.

The realization that there really is no "self" underneath the story line can actually be very liberating. The idea (and experience) of "no story, no self" can help us recognize the transitory quality of our identity, and challenge our assumptions about who we actually are. What's left when our usual story-line is inevitably disrupted?

Try this:

Go inside, and remind yourself of a familiar story: I'm so this or I'm so that. Then allow your attention to shift toward a simple awareness of telling yourself a story. Let the story fade as you pay more attention to the awareness itself. What's it like to let these ideas go? Just experience this moment, letting the usual story run in the background, if it's still there, but not getting hooked into it.

As we let go of these various stories of who we thought we were, there's an amazing spaciousness. That's what we really are, aside from all the usual commentary. And that's the sense in which there really is no "self" that we need to hang on to: we don't need to believe our own (or anyone else's) obsessive accounts of who we are. We can also discover what it's like when we just make a note of the usual story, but don't indulge it.

This can also be a bit disorienting, and even frightening for some people! Who am I now, if I'm not operating according to all my usual stories, expected roles, and sense of self?

However, when we clear out the old story line, we're more likely to get in touch with what's truly distinctive about our own lives. We each have our own natural unfolding that's unique in all the world, that has never been seen before, and will never be seen again. Yet there's no reason to grasp on to it. Grasping only makes us all the less likely to express our true nature.

We can release ourselves from all the negative conditioning we've accrued over many decades by shifting our attention from the story line to what's happening right now, in this moment.

We could call this ongoing awareness your true Self, your higher Self, or even Self-realization: that which is beyond all the stories we tell ourselves. And that's the paradoxical secret to true self-esteem—there's no need to counter poor self-esteem by pumping yourself up with affirmations, or by trying to develop "high" self-esteem—it's almost as though the question of self-esteem becomes irrelevant. You simply exist, like a blossoming flower, without having to question (or justify) your *beingness*.

Consider the lilies of the field, how they grow: they toil not, neither do they spin.

—Jesus, *Sermon on the Mount*

Humility without Humiliation

Pride goeth before destruction,
And a haughty spirit before a fall.

—*Proverbs*

Both pride and low self-esteem are based on the assumption that you need to defend yourself. Pride is often an attempt to counter low self-esteem, and low self-esteem is frequently the result of pride being punctured. An exaggerated self-importance is easily deflated. Whereas humility doesn't puff itself up, because we're not trying to prove anything: it's simply a more accurate assessment of our true abilities. Then we're less vulnerable to humiliation, and we're more likely to develop genuine self-confidence.

More and more, you begin to recognize your true Self in the unconditioned: that very subtle part of your moment-to-moment experience which is not operating according to how you've been hurt, who you think you are, living up to others' expectations, or how you judge yourself.

Try this:

Go inside for a moment, and take in a deep breath. Allow yourself to get in touch with that moment-to-moment experience of awareness. What are you aware of now? And now there's a new moment: now I'm aware of: (fill in the blank).

If we can come back to our core self, our true nature, or just an awareness of our own body, most of the time, we're fine. Yes, we may come up with various projects we'd like to accomplish, and ways we'd like to take care of ourselves. If these are a natural outgrowth of our own unique unfolding, our own delight in being in the world, they can be wonderful expressions of who we are.

Having realized his own self as the Self, a man becomes selfless.
—*Maitrayana Upanishad*

CHAPTER 3

THE POWER OF MINDFULNESS

CALM, STEADY, AND CLEAR

The ultimate truth is so simple: it is nothing more than being in one's natural, original state.
—Ramana Maharshi

Wouldn't it be nice to settle your mind into a relaxed state, any time you wanted to? That's the natural state of our minds, when we're no longer caught in the vortex of our negative conditioning!

Getting beyond such reactivity may seem like an impossible task, yet most of us have already had a glimpse of this lovely sense of being "all right in the world." It may have been as simple as reflecting a baby's smile, seeing a sunset, or feeling a summer's breeze on a balmy evening. We've all experienced this, even if it didn't register as anything extraordinary.

And that's partly the point: whistles don't have to go off, no fireworks or explosions need to announce the arrival of this awareness. Rather, it's very calm, steady, and clear, without any striving or grasping.

In this chapter, we'll look at various ways to become more mindful of the present moment. Practicing mindfulness, in turn, will increase your ability to catch yourself when you get caught in that negative vortex. Then you can shift your mood with even greater ease.

Mindfulness for the Klutz

He lived at a little distance from his body.
—James Joyce, from "A Painful Case," *Dubliners*

Although the practice of mindfulness is often seen as a path to spiritual awakening, my own journey was prompted by a practical motivation: simply to move through the world more easily, without clunking my head, barking my shin, biting my cheek, or stubbing my toe.

Most kids discover early on: if you don't watch where you're going, you're likely to get bruised. I guess I'm a slow learner; it took me a while to make the connection between my lack of attention and bumping into things! I was frequently so absorbed in my own thoughts, that I didn't pay much attention to where I was going. So I was initially attracted to mindfulness out of a simple desire for self-preservation. (I could have used something like *Mindfulness for the Klutz, Space Cadet, or the Absent-Minded.*)

Although I had read some books on meditation in college, my introduction to the practice of mindfulness was during the summer of 1974 at the Naropa Institute in Boulder, Colorado. It was quite a summer! Chögyam Trungpa and Ram Dass taught in large lecture halls. Allen Ginsberg read his poetry along with Anne Waldman and Diane di Prima in a packed auditorium. Joseph Goldstein and Jack

Kornfield offered instruction in *Vipassana*, a form of insight meditation. I was in a practice seminar with Joseph, who taught us how to pay attention to each moment as it arises.

What a concept! Being mindful helped me pay closer attention not only to my own mind, but also to where I was going. As I grew more adept at locating myself in space, I became less likely to collide with my surroundings.

When I became a psychotherapist, mindfulness greatly enhanced my work with clients. As I slowed down enough to be aware of the present moment, I also became more sensitive to physical changes in the people I worked with. I could track shifts in mood, agitation levels, or even longing, because I was able to identify these shifts in myself, as well.

I suspect the heart of that longing is a wish to simply *be* in the world. When we relax into the present moment, the details of our daily drama and current hassles tend to feel far less compelling.

Mindfulness also enhances an awareness of our natural unfolding. At the same time, we develop a greater choice about how we'd rather live: in the tension of our previous conditioning, or in the relaxed awareness of the present moment?

By challenging the usual stories we tell ourselves, mindfulness can help us have a direct experience that we're not just our thoughts, roles, or stories; and we don't have to be enslaved by fluctuating moods. Mindfulness allows us to dwell in the spaciousness that arises when we're not swept up by the passing storm.

Mindful awareness also enables us to experience insights as an *embodied consciousness*, which seems to facilitate emotional growth and healing by engaging an awareness of our bodies, as well as our minds.

What Is Mindfulness?

"Mindfulness means paying attention in a particular way: on purpose, in the present moment, and non-judgmentally."
—Jon Kabat-Zinn

Mindfulness is simply a method to help us become more aware of what's actually going on in any given moment. This awareness allows us to expand our choices about where we'd rather direct our attention. Paying attention to the present moment can enhance our sense of wonder and awe, simply at being alive. It can inspire gratitude, loving kindness, compassion, joy, and a greater sense of ease in the world.

Mindfulness has a rich history in contemplative traditions as a vital part of spiritual awakening; however, the practice of mindfulness doesn't require any specific religious beliefs. I see it as a practical, down-to-earth way to heal from previous wounds, follow through on our best intentions, and get in touch with our own wisdom. Naturally, years of practice can lead to greater depth, but the fruits of mindfulness are easily within reach of anyone who pays attention for even a moment.

The purpose of mindfulness is to develop stability in our chaotic minds, so that we're not so vulnerable to being hijacked by every passing thought, feeling, reaction, or mood. *This calm stability can help us perceive reality without the distortions of our previous conditioning.* This in turn can lead to vitality, freedom, and aliveness. Then we can bring this clarity to whatever we experience: in work, love, or simply following our natural interests.

Because we're no longer reacting to our own distortions, mindfulness can generate confidence even in difficult circumstances. We're able to be more responsive to the world around us. This responsiveness actually provides us a great deal of freedom, which at first can be unsettling: if I'm no longer reacting out of my usual habits, how do I make choices? Why would I even bother to do anything at all?

Being free of our previous conditioning doesn't mean we no longer care. In fact, seeing into the true nature of reality, we realize that we have a lot in common with our fellow beings in the world. We're all just trying to get along the best we can, and this realization can help us develop deep compassion, common cause, and even loving kindness toward our neighbors.

As human beings, we often tend toward tribalism, so our empathy may be limited to our own families, ethnic group, or nation. When we were isolated hunter-gatherers, clinging to our own tribe had some survival value. Yet now, with an interconnected world—facing global warming, an energy crisis, scarcity of resources, epidemics, and war—we can no longer afford to indulge in tribalism.

Stability and clarity lead to a greater understanding that we're all in this together. This recognition of our common humanity can help us get in touch with our own natural fellow-feeling and open-hearted compassion.

I believe that extending this compassion to encompass the entire world is *the* major task of humanity. By becoming mindful, we can become less suspicious and more gracious, generous, and compassionate. Each of us, in our own small way, can contribute to making this a more livable world that can sustain us all.

Twelve Benefits of Mindfulness

Since the 1980s, the *Mind and Life Institute* has sponsored a series of dialogues between neuroscientists and the Dalai

Lama, demonstrating the benefits of practice. Mindfulness not only enables us to be more present, it's also becoming increasingly clear from various studies that moment-to-moment awareness can increase emotional well-being in numerous ways. Here are some of the benefits I've experienced in my own practice:

1. *Being in the present*

Mindfulness cultivates your awareness of the present moment, which can help you feel more alive and attuned to your surroundings.

2. *Deep appreciation*

As you become more present, you may see things as if for the first time. You become acutely aware of the profound depth of all your senses: the beauty of branches against a starry sky, the fragrance of a spring rain, the taste of a crisp apple, the music of a bird's song, or the pleasure of a warm embrace.

3. *Reduced stress*

Mindfulness helps you relax, and counters any tendencies you may have to become uptight or anxious.

4. *More accepting*

As you become more relaxed, you can "go with the flow" and deal with whatever life throws at you with greater ease.

5. *Clarity*

You begin to see and understand situations as they actually are, not simply through the filter of your previous expectations.

6. *Wisdom*
As you gain more clarity, you'll develop wiser choices about how you want to respond.

7. *Release old patterns*
As you become gentler with yourself and others, you can gradually let go of previous patterns that no longer serve you.

8. *Loving kindness, compassion, and empathy*
As you develop more understanding of your own internal process, you'll naturally feel more compassion for yourself as well as others.

9. *Generosity*
Feeling more connected to others increases your generosity: not only with money and material objects, but also by giving more freely of yourself.

10. *Confidence and trust*
You'll develop more confidence in your own abilities, increasing trust in both yourself and others.

11. *Luminosity, presence, and being*
As you settle into the present moment, these qualities seem to arise spontaneously: seeing things clearly, and being present without forcing an agenda—see what arises when you are simply *being*.

12. *Spiritual awakening and grace*
Awakening to the present has a lovely quality of grace, ease, and just-rightness in the moment.

How to Become More Mindful

Every moment of mindfulness renounces the reflexive, self-protecting response of the mind in favor of clear and balanced understanding.

—Sylvia Boorstein

Mindful awareness of the present moment gives you a choice: would you rather engage in moment-to-moment awareness, or be trapped in the vortex of your negative conditioning?

Mindfulness helps us calm agitation, stabilize our attention, and develop self-compassion. Here's a helpful resource, from The Wellspring Institute for Neuroscience and Contemplative Wisdom at www.wisebrain.org. Rick Hanson and Rick Mendius have provided guided meditations and a wealth of information about integrating neuroscience with contemplative practice.

They offer five "Foundations of Meditation," which set the stage for mindfulness practice by calming our reactivity:

1. Set an intention.
2. Relax your body.
3. Feel safe.
4. Evoke positive emotion.
5. Recognize and absorb the benefits.

By setting an intention, we can ease into our experience, which helps us relax and feel safer, without the anticipation of danger that often floods through us. Then we're more likely to evoke positive emotion, and absorb the benefits that arise from calming and soothing our agitated, over-re-active system.

They also identify seven "Basics of Meditation" that explain in very simple terms how to meditate:

1. Relax.
2. Find a posture that is comfortable and alert.
3. Have good will toward yourself.
4. Become aware of your body.
5. Focus on something (such as your breath) to steady your attention.
6. Accept whatever passes through awareness, not resist-ing it or chasing it.
7. Gently settle into peaceful well-being.

This next section will give you a taste of what it's like to simply be aware of the present moment, along with a few suggestions for monitoring your experience. I'll be using an example of sitting meditation, but we can also become more mindful doing any activity: when we're walking, eating, stand-ing in line at the check-out counter, or even caught in traffic!

When I sit down to meditate, I often light a candle and ring a bell, just to provide myself a way of setting aside this moment as a special time and place. The flame of a candle regenerates itself in every moment—the same as you! It's a lovely reminder that we can re-awaken with each breath.

If you already have a spiritual practice, you may want to include whatever resonates with your own aspirations: per-haps a picture of a religious figure you admire, a sacred text, or a quote that inspires you.

I have found it helpful to take in a series of deep breaths, just to relax and bring myself into the present moment, setting aside all of the other thoughts, plans, and activities of the day. Then I remind myself of my intention, which also serves the purpose of helping me feel more relaxed, calm, and safe. I happen to feel drawn to the *Divine Abodes*: loving kindness, compassion, joy, and equanimity (or ease). Catholics might recite the rosary, and Protestants might be drawn to the Lord's Prayer, for example. You may have your own favorite prayer, poem, or verse from Hindu, Jewish, Buddhist, Sufi, or earth-centered traditions that reminds you of some quality you'd like to cultivate in your life, and perhaps dedicate this moment of mindfulness to that hope or wish.

Or, if you don't identify with any particular spiritual tradition, you can simply aspire to be calm, centered, and present: may I be safe, happy, and well—may all beings be happy and live with ease! These aspirations can fill you with positive emotion.

Then I'll focus for a while on my natural breath, and gradually shift to simply monitoring whatever arises, developing an awareness of impermanence, not getting caught up in my passing dramas, settling into a sense of well-being, and occasionally having an insight that we're all connected (see chapter 8: STEEPED IN GRACE).

Try this:

Take in a deep breath and let it go. Just follow the natural rhythm of your breath, in and out, without having to force anything. You may find it helpful to count your breaths from one to ten (or backwards, from ten to one), just as a way to monitor your attention. Try this for three minutes, and just see what happens.

This simple exercise can be very revealing about the nature of our minds! We realize we may not be in as much control of our conscious awareness as we thought we were, as we lose track of our breath, lose track of counting, and drift off. So part of the idea is to maintain our awareness of what's coming up, without being distracted by the actual content of each succeeding thought or impression.

From Ram Dass's *Be Here Now* to Eckhart Tolle's *The Power of Now*, much has been made in recent years about being in the "now," cultivating and appreciating the present moment. Being present can release us from the usual tension of our conditioning. In his books and retreats, Alan Wallace reminds us that the Pali word *sati*, which is often translated as "mindfulness" or "present awareness," also means *remembering* to be mindful, as a way of monitoring the quality of our attention.

Mindfulness can help us monitor our agitation level, so we're more likely to catch ourselves when we're getting uptight. We can also gain more steadiness in our awareness by noticing when we're spacing out. This balance has traditionally been compared to tuning the strings of a lute or a guitar—not too tight, and not too loose—as we get in touch with the music of our own awakening, and tap into our inner resources when we get caught up in our reactivity.

By being mindful, we can become more aware of grasping and aversion—what we want more of, what we want less of—and how we can be more satisfied in the present moment. Of course, part of awareness is a natural responsiveness: your foot's going to sleep, so you shift your position. You're thirsty, so you have a drink of water. This natural responsiveness is not what we mean by grasping or aversion. Grasping is when you're caught by an intense desire to have your own way no matter what, which often leads to acute suffering! Whereas, responsiveness is the ability to respond in a natural way to current circumstances, without the reactivity that arises from previous negative conditioning.

While meditating for more than a few minutes, it's easy to fall into a spacey-sort of dullness, especially if you're tired. Given the lack of sleep that many of us experience in our hectic lives, it's a common experience! You can arouse your attention by becoming more aware of your body in the present moment. Open your eyes, and look upwards slightly. You can also stand up, swing your arms, and take in a number of quick breaths. And, of course, if you're really tired, sometimes it's helpful just to take a nap, and try again later.

Other times, you may feel incredibly restless, your thoughts bouncing all over the place, like a hyper-active monkey jumping from one branch to another! You can release agitation and lessen your restlessness by lowering your gaze, taking in a deep breath, and letting it go.

Try this:
Look around the room, and say to yourself:
Now I'm aware of: (fill in the blank).
And again: Now I'm aware of:
Go all around the room, and just observe in each moment the object of your awareness, repeating this phrase each time you shift your attention: Now I'm aware of:
Then bring it back to yourself, and the sounds you're aware of. Then bring your attention to your breath, how it moves in and out. If you're very quiet, you may even feel

your own heartbeat. There it goes, pumping away from before you were born until the last moment of your life, seemingly all on its own. Feel sensations: what it's like to be sitting where you are, the pressure on your legs and against your back; any tastes, smells, or sounds. What's happening in this moment; and now this? Thoughts, plans, and judgments arise and pass away. Notice how your attention shifts, moment-to-moment. Allow yourself to be in touch with the awareness that's still there, even as thoughts, images, memories, and sensations come and go.

Thinking Is Not Your Enemy

"Every time we become aware of a thought, as opposed to being lost in a thought, we experience that opening of the mind."
—Joseph Goldstein

Thinking is not an "enemy" of mindful awareness; we can simply observe thoughts arising and passing away. Sometimes they come in torrents, other times barely a trickle. We can note them with "bare attention," like clouds passing by, and let them go.

Thoughts can also be a natural, creative response to our current circumstances. I discovered that persistent thoughts, or even "great ideas" and creative insights lose their hold if I jot them down. Then it's easier to let them go and gently bring my awareness back to the present moment.

Every thought, sensation, memory, or even painful emotion can be "grist for the mill." The point of mindfulness is not to stop the flow of activity in our minds, but simply to become more mindful of the flow itself, rather than getting caught up in the content of each passing thought, impulse, or impression. This doesn't have to be all somber and serious; make a game of it, like you're on the look-out for the next thought that arises: what's it going to be? How curious! We realize we're not really in that much control of whatever comes down the pike.

Interestingly enough, by shifting our attention to the flow of our minds, instead of getting caught by the content, eventually that flow begins to slow down. From a rushing waterfall of cascading thoughts, it turns into a river, meandering into a lake, where it finally comes to rest: like a calm, clear pool.

Paying attention develops your awareness and enhances steadiness, which can lead to a glimpse of clarity: even an awareness of *awareness itself!*

These moments of clarity are tempting to hold on to, yet each moment follows the next, complete in itself—no holding on to the last moment, no yearning for the next—just being totally present with whatever is happening right now, and trusting your own responsiveness.

At the end of your meditation session, even if your mind jumped all over the place, gently remind yourself once again of your intention to relax, be calmer, and appreciate your efforts. (See the APPENDIX, for another guided mindfulness.)

Active Mindfulness

We are near awakening when we dream that we dream.
—Novalis

Nightmares provide a common example of how easy it is to get caught in delusional thinking. While a nightmare is taking place, it seems very real, and unless you're having a lucid dream, you're not aware that you're only dreaming. But when you wake up, you realize it was all just a dream; there's no real monster chasing you. Although it can be interesting to look at what the dream signifies, you're not stuck in it.

Similarly, other memories and automatic reactions are simply old patterns. When you shift out of the pattern, it doesn't "exist" in quite the same way. Since it's no longer activated, *you don't have to go there!* You may get sucked back into that vortex, but mindfulness can help you realize this sooner than later, and you can *shift your mood* to climb back out again.

Shifting your mood through **FIRE** Wisdom is an active form of mindfulness that can help you catch yourself in unproductive habits of thought (or neural pathways). Then you can shift to your own source of contentment, well-being, and wisdom. You're more likely to decide what you want to do next, based on your natural growth and what seems like a helpful and productive step.

So we begin to have more of a choice about where we want to locate ourselves. We can focus on what's lacking, which is fine if it truly motivates taking action. But if you just get demoralized, you can get in touch with how that registers in your body: just notice how you feel, physically.

Then instead of pulling away from the tension, actually go into it, crank it up, and feel how you make it tighter. As you've already experienced, if you can make it tighter, you can allow it to loosen. So ease off, and notice how you relax yourself. Your body knows how to do this! Crank it up a notch, and note the contrast. Now crank it up again, hold your breath—hold it, hold it, hold it—then let it go. Release your breath, and let all parts of your body relax.

Then, from this more relaxed place, tell that tense part of yourself what you know now, about how to handle whatever situation you're faced with.

FIRE Wisdom offers an antidote to your conditioning by recognizing your reactivity, intensifying the tension, and then releasing. You can then move into the source of your own love and inner wisdom.

Altered Traits

In their book *Altered Traits*, Daniel Goleman and Richard Davidson have documented the persistence of traits that transcend momentary states in advanced mindfulness practitioners. These include the ability to sustain attention, and becoming less reactive to stress. With consistent practice, we can become more aware of the nature of existence: how everything changes, we can't always get what we want, and how not to take disappointments so personally. This allows us to be more at ease in our daily lives, appreciating the aliveness of one moment after another.

Penetrative insight, joined with calm abiding, utterly eradicates afflicted states.

—Shantideva

CHAPTER 4

WHEN THE GOING GETS TOUGH

THE TOUGH KEEP COOL

When we meet real tragedy in life, we can react in two ways: either by losing hope and falling into self-destructive habits, or by using the challenge to find our inner strength.

—Dalai Lama

We've seen how we're not just our thoughts, roles, or stories; and we don't have to be hijacked by fluctuating moods. In this chapter, we'll look at some strategies for keeping your cool even in the face of hard times and difficult challenges.

The Pali word *dukkha*, often translated as "suffering," originally meant "out of alignment," like a wheel out of kilter on an axle. Various aspects in our lives can easily go "out of kilter." When we cling to a specific outcome of how each moment is supposed to unfold, we suffer. Yet when we can simply respond to developments in an open-hearted way, we become re-aligned with this moment, even if it's difficult, and figure out what we want to do next.

This may seem easier said than done, especially when we're filled with adrenalin from anger or fear. In her book, *My Stroke of Insight*, neuroanatomist Jill Bolte Taylor says it takes less than ninety seconds for that initial storm to pass. In the meantime, it's helpful to "count to ten" before responding, so we don't simply lash out.

How can we deal with tough situations in a way that doesn't make them worse? Mindfulness can help us remember what else is possible: the larger perspective that helps keep us from giving up, retaliating, or acting out. Then shifting your mood can help you access a calmer, wiser choice of how you'd like to respond.

Being mindful doesn't mean passively accepting negative developments. Most of our classic stories show the hero surmounting obstacles in order to reach a goal. Rather than wallowing in disappointment, wishing things were different, the hero rises to the occasion with ever greater perseverance and ingenuity.

Hassles at Work

When Jack first came to see me, he was very upset by how he was being treated at work, a non-profit agency serving homeless people in the Tenderloin neighborhood of San Francisco. They provide temporary housing, food vouchers, and counseling to help clients get back on their feet.

Jack's main complaint was that he got mixed messages from a co-worker named Don, who was in control of assigning intakes. At the shelter, there was frequent confusion about whose responsibility it was to follow up after the intake. Yet Don seemed to interpret Jack's attempt to clarify their roles as if he were trying to shirk his responsibility. During staff meetings, Don said how much he "admired" Jack for taking care of himself, since "Jack always makes sure he doesn't work too hard." But Jack saw himself as very conscientious in the service of their mission, so Don's sarcasm really annoyed him.

Consequently, to avoid blowing up at Don during staff meetings, Jack would shut down. He felt depressed, without much energy, and anxious every time he anticipated another run-in with Don.

He could have quit his job, but he actually enjoyed working with his clients. He also felt he was making a real difference in their lives. So he wanted to see if there was a better way to handle these conflicts at work.

I asked him to go inside, and get in touch with how these various encounters and feelings were registering in his body. He felt pretty tense in his chest and shoulders. When I asked him what associations came up for him, he remembered being in the car with his father when he was around nine years old. His father was drunk, and driving erratically. Jack was holding on for dear life, and pleaded with his dad to slow down. His father exploded at him: "You wimp, you little wuss. Don't you ever talk back to me that way again!" Just then, he jumped the curb and slammed into a telephone pole. They were both shaken up, but luckily they weren't seriously injured. Nonetheless, his father yelled at Jack: "See what you made me do!"

As a young child, Jack understandably developed a deeply ingrained assumption that he wasn't safe. It wasn't okay to disclose your fear, or you'd be attacked, belittled, and demeaned. He concluded that if he speaks up he might even get killed, and he's powerless to do anything about it. Instead of simply seeing that his father had a serious problem, he concluded that there must be something basically wrong with him. Why else would his father treat him this way?

Jack could now see that his interactions with Don elicited this entire sequence of feelings, reactions, and conclusions about the danger of speaking up in difficult situations.

Before dealing directly with either his past or his current conflict, we paused for a moment to see if we could help him gain access to his own inner source of safety.

"Go inside for a moment, and imagine a place somewhere in your past where you felt safe, warm, and welcome; if there was any spot that really felt like home to you."

Jack was able to identify a place of safety for himself: when he was ten, he dug a fort in his backyard, reinforced by plywood and two-by-fours. He felt powerful there, and secure from any invaders.

"How smart you were, to find your own way to protect yourself. This is a wonderful resource you can always come back to. Feel the security and power of being in this fort you built with your own hands. What do you know from inside your fort, about what was going on with your family?"

"They were messed up; my dad was an alcoholic, my mother was in denial and wouldn't ever stand up to him. I was just a little kid in a powerless situation."

I had him go back inside, and asked him "Knowing what you know now, what would like to tell your father?"

"You're a drunk, and you're scaring me, and it's not okay. That's not how you should treat your own son. You're not being a good parent. You should get some help!" Jack had tears streaming down his cheeks.

I said "It's really sad there was nobody in your life who could take care of you, protect you, or intervene with your family. You went through a lot, having to endure this messed-up situation until you were old enough to escape. In the meantime, you did the best you could to keep yourself safe, and avoid making things worse."

As we explored the connection between his early experiences and his current situation at work, he got in touch with an amazing amount of tension he was holding in his body. When he remembered Don making disparaging remarks about him, his body went rigid. I had him go into it, feeling the sensations and whatever associations came with it, crank it up, take in a deep breath, and let it go. Then he got in touch with a greater perspective about the dynamics between them: "These interactions with Don trigger how powerless I felt with my father. But I can remind myself that I'm safe now, and I can express my own point of view."

Over the next few weeks, Jack was gradually able to separate his fear of getting killed from what was actually happening at work. He felt more comfortable speaking up when there was confusion about his assignments. Even if Don got defensive, Jack was not as likely to feel threatened. He could monitor the tension that arose in his body, then relax. He was able to stay with the facts of the case, and assert his perspective about what services they should provide. Even though he never really trusted Don, they eventually were able to work out a more peaceful co-existence. He even found that over time he gained some allies at work who could see his point about various procedures. He felt good about some changes the agency made in response to his suggestions.

Jack developed his ability to recognize when he was getting caught in his previous pattern of feeling threatened. While it made sense that he wanted to challenge dysfunctional dynamics at work, he no longer felt controlled by his previous reactions. He gradually realized that the level of danger he perceived at work was out of proportion to the actual situation, so he could get in touch with what he really needed. This gave him the freedom to deal with work conflicts more assertively, without exploding, quitting, or shutting down.

Road Rage!

If we learn to open our hearts, anyone, including the people who drive us crazy, can be our teacher.

—Pema Chödrön

How many of us, even if we'd like to see ourselves as pretty balanced with most of our lives, nonetheless "lose it" in traffic when someone cuts us off, jumps a four-way stop, or otherwise drives in a manner that seems inconsiderate, selfish, or even dangerous?

My pet peeve is when someone's turning left at an intersection in front of me, but they don't pull up far enough for the next car to get around them. So you're stuck behind them until they make the turn, at which point the light turns red and you have to wait for another signal. Rats! They should post signs at every intersection reminding drivers to pull up and let other cars get around you!

See how I get? And I'll bet anything that you have things that drive you crazy about other people's driving, as well.

This is a fairly minor example of everyday annoyances, yet it's often these petty aggravations that really get to us. However, if we can learn to relax even when things get "out of kilter," we can live more gracefully, and be better prepared for major disappointments.

So how can we do it? One way is to realize that not everyone is a perfect driver, even if we wish they were. Another is to recognize, with some humility, that maybe we're not always a perfect driver, ourselves. Recently I was so intent on checking traffic coming from my left so I could make a right turn, that I didn't notice a pedestrian starting into the crosswalk from my right. He banged on my hood and shouted "Stop!"

I figure we're all trying to get somewhere, so I try wishing us well: may we all get where we're going—on time if possible—but if not, at least safely. I'd rather be late, than get into an accident!

Recently I was crossing the Golden Gate Bridge, and the car in front of me was only going thirty miles per hour in a forty-five zone. With traffic speeding by on my left, I couldn't pass him. When we finally got off the bridge, he took the exit toward Sausalito. I felt relieved, and sped up—but then he suddenly veered back into my lane, still going thirty, so I had to slam on my brakes. I beeped my horn, then changed lanes to get around him.

About a mile later, I saw a car looming in my rearview mirror, so I changed lanes to let him get by. Then he came right up next to me, and I could see it was the same guy. He veered his car into my lane, only inches away, scowling at me. I moved over, trying not to swerve, then slowed way down to let him pass me by. He sped ahead of me and took the next off-ramp.

I think part of the problem with road-rage is that we're encased in these huge metal contraptions that prevent us from having a more humane interaction. On crowded streets, if we bump into each other we can just say "excuse me," and the other person can tell from our quick apology and tone of voice that we weren't being purposely hostile or rude. But from inside our cars, we don't have that personal connection, and we tend to over-react.

Here's another way of looking at traffic that I've used to calm myself:

If you were trekking through the jungle, and you saw an elephant on the rampage, you probably wouldn't get mad at the elephant; the elephant is just being a crazed elephant, and when they get that way, they go on rampages. So you think, uh-oh, danger; let's keep out of that elephant's way! Or if you saw a tiger prowling for dinner, you wouldn't get mad at the tiger, you'd just be very cautious. If you saw a huge boa constrictor hanging from a tree, or a cobra rearing up to strike, you'd do the best you could to make your way safely around it.

Similarly, you see some crazed driver careening down the highway, zipping in and out of lanes, cutting you off. You could get annoyed and gun your engine to catch up with him or flip him off, thereby putting not only him, but yourself and everyone else on the road in danger. Or you could say to yourself, "Whoa, there goes someone in a mad rush, think I'll pull back and stay out of their way."

And be glad that you're not as crazed as he is, by taking in a deep breath, and relax your tension. Maybe even wish him well, that he gets where he's going in such an obvious hurry, and that we all get where we're going safely.

I find that waving someone ahead of me or giving a nod to a pedestrian often allows me to feel more generous. I don't always have to insist on my "right" of way, even if others are taking an unfair advantage. In the grand scheme of things, what different does it make if I get where I'm going a few moments later? With a friendly wave, there's a momentary appreciation and recognition that we're all in this together, and I usually feel better about myself, as well.

A friend of mine once told his son how frustrated he felt when they got stuck in traffic while inching their way toward the toll plaza to cross the Bay Bridge. "Doesn't it bother you?" he asked. His son, who was nine at the time, seemed fairly content as he peered out the window. He turned and said "No, I like to watch all the different cars and trucks going by."

He didn't have the same sense of urgency as his father, which allowed him to have a different experience. Instead of feeling "stuck," he was fascinated by the different sizes and shapes of the cars and trucks converging on the toll plaza.

This example doesn't mean we shouldn't have any opinions about traffic, or other difficulties. Feelings are natural responses that can motivate action. Irritation with congestion could inspire support for mass transit, for example. But when we're stuck in it, being aggravated for over an hour doesn't really contribute anything to the solution, and can actually make us more likely to get into an accident.

I try to remember that getting caught in traffic or not making a signal is simply another opportunity to stop for a moment, take a deep breath, and practice being mindful during this pause in my travels. I can look around, listen to music, and even feel grateful that I'm making my way safely across town.

Fellow-feeling, Even for Strangers

Compassion for me is just what the word says: it is "suffering with." It is an immediate participation in the suffering of another to such a degree that you forget yourself and your own safety and spontaneously do what is necessary.

—Joseph Campbell

Despite our annoyance with people making dangerous choices in traffic, or even holding up the line at the grocery store, we also have an amazing capacity for immediate empathy that transcends our usual categories of people we're close to.

In the midst of a true catastrophe—when someone's life is in real danger—we may suddenly thrust ourselves into the breach to take care of them, as if they were our own souls. We see this all the time in response to natural disasters, such as the tsunami in the Indian Ocean several years ago, earthquakes, fires, mudslides, floods, and hurricanes. We also saw it in the heroic response to the 9/11 attacks on the World Trade Center, where people spontaneously extended themselves to others in need.

Joseph Campbell tells the story of a policeman rescuing an attempted suicide from the Pali cliff on the island of Oahu. The policeman caught him just as he was going over the ledge, yet soon found himself in danger of being pulled over by the weight of the young man. But instead of letting go, he struggled to hold on to him. As he was dragged closer to the edge, his partner suddenly grabbed him and pulled them both back from the precipice.

When asked why he held on to this stranger, even at risk to his own life, he said "I couldn't let go. If I had let that young man go, I couldn't have lived another day of my life!"

This transcendence of self-concern is an instantaneous expression of our mutual connection.

What about Grief?

When you are sorrowful look again in your heart,
and you shall see that in truth you are weeping
for that which has been your delight.

—Kahlil Gibran

If we can feel this mutual caring even for strangers, it's no wonder that we're often devastated by the loss of someone we love.

When confronted with real adversity—natural disasters, life-threatening illness, disability, or the death of a loved one—it's only natural that we would respond with shock, sadness, and mourning. We are social beings, with real attachment to others, and we are severely affected by significant loss.

It's important to allow our feelings to flow through us, and not try to stop them out of some misguided notion that we wouldn't be affected if we weren't so "attached." Recent studies suggest that emotional connections actually help regulate our physiology, as well as our emotional lives. As the story above from Joseph Campbell demonstrates, this capacity for feeling connected to others is really what makes us human.

Leaping to premature closure for our grief can be understood as a *spiritual bypass:* we have some idealized notion of non-attachment in mind, and think that's how we should react, regardless of how we actually feel. Some people think they should keep a stiff upper lip and try not to be affected by a significant loss. Emotional connections are both normal and healthy, and the forced suppression of grief can lead to prolonged depression.

At the same time, it's helpful to challenge pessimistic assumptions about our future in response to our loss. *Feel whatever you feel, but don't leap to unrealistic conclusions.* Take each day as it comes, feel into the nature of the changes you are facing, be willing to discover the next step that makes sense to you, rather than jumping to the conclusion that all is lost. It's also helpful to reach out for support from others, to assuage your grief, and to be reminded of others' caring.

Can there be serenity, even in grief? I think so, but not as an ideal to measure ourselves against. Just notice what happens when you allow your emotions to flow through you, without running any story line about what it all means for the future. There can be a profound mourning of our loss, that feels comforting and meaningful.

Turn Regrets into Inspiration

Significant loss often reminds us of regrets: what we wish we could have expressed or done instead. Yet we can't turn back the clock; whatever we wish we could have done, it's impossible to recreate previous circumstances. However, rather than banging ourselves over the head with recrimination, we can use our regrets to inspire future action.

Try this:

Go inside, and get in touch with something you feel some regret about. What do you wish you could have done or said? If it's still possible to make amends, what would that look like for you? What does your regret suggest about how you want to live now?

By transforming regret into inspiration, we're more likely to forgive ourselves. And forgiving ourselves can help us develop compassion for others: we're all fallible human beings, each acting out of our own conditioning, yet gradually developing our ability to catch ourselves by becoming more mindful of each moment.

This inspiration can serve as a source of fresh ideas for re-engagement, which often allows us to focus on what's possible, rather than dwelling on the past. We gradually develop our capacity to re-enter the everyday world. We become clearer about where we'd like to go, what we'd like to do. And just as significantly, we can get in touch with how we would like to *be* in the world with this new perspective, not just what we can accomplish.

Physical Pain

Pain is inevitable. Suffering is optional.

—M. Kathleen Casey

This is a hard one for me, as I do everything I can to avoid pain. When I'm in physical pain, it's hard for me to believe that I have any choice at all about my suffering!

I once had strep throat that was so bad that every time I swallowed, I cringed. I felt sick, weak, and feverish. Then it turned into a kidney infection, and my lower back was wracked with pain. Every position I switched to did nothing to relieve it, as I tossed back and forth.

My own internal protest that this should not be happening didn't seem to help much. In fact, my wish that it wasn't happening only seemed to make it worse. I was finally treated with antibiotics and a strong pain-reliever, but it took a while for them to kick in. I got to a point where I finally gave up resisting the pain, and simply became aware of the tiniest gaps between throbs. I tried as much as possible to relax into it as the medication gradually provided some relief.

As I'm writing this, I have a sore shoulder from over-exertion. It's been going on for several weeks now, and I finally went to the doctor to see if something was out of joint. I'm hopeful that it will soon repair itself, but in the meantime, I'm taking care of it with cold packs, and by not straining myself. I'm also trying to shift my attention back to work, enjoying small pleasures even with my limited range of movement.

I don't think enduring pain is easy for anyone. Aside from being rear-ended a few times, I've been very fortunate in my life not to have experienced serious accidents, major illness, or chronic bouts of unrelenting pain. People who have learned to live with chronic pain and various disabilities are incredible role-models of how to make the best of difficult situations.

The Pain Research Forum sponsors a website at http://relief.news, which has a wealth of recent articles for dealing with pain. Jon Kabat-Zinn's book *Full Catastrophe Living: Using the Wisdom of Your Body and Mind to Face Stress, Pain and Illness* is another great resource to help people cope more effectively with pain. He developed this approach through the University of Massachusetts Medical School's Stress Reduction Program. (Mindfulness Based Stress Reduction is now being offered in many centers throughout the country. Search the internet for classes in your local area.)

I think a large part of the success of this mindfulness-based approach is that it enables us to relax, and increases our ability to shift our attention slightly, so we're not totally consumed by our pain.

One strategy is to focus on your physical sensations, looking for *tiny gaps* in the pulses of pain; and the other is to divert your attention, and *shift your focus* to other things: being with loved ones, children, and pets; shifting your attention toward work or creative activities; even watching funny movies seems to help! It's not just the pain that causes our suffering, but the tension that arises from cursing our fate, which only seems to make it worse.

Some recent research has shown that painful reactions can sometimes perpetuate themselves. No matter what the original source of our pain was, our nerves can get overly-sensitized to a recurring pattern of anticipation and reactivity, so that we continue to feel pain even after there's no longer any organic cause for it. This "reflex sympathetic dystrophy" (also known as "complex regional pain syndrome") can be incredibly frustrating to deal with, especially if medical professionals aren't familiar with this condition. They may assume that you're malingering, or it's "all in your head." However, there are some treatments being developed to help deal with nerves that become hyper-sensitized in this way.

There have been great strides in the medical treatment of pain. If you're experiencing chronic pain, get evaluated by a pain management specialist so you can obtain whatever treatments are available for your condition.

The Wounded Healer

Turn your wounds into wisdom.

—Oprah Winfrey

The concept of the "wounded healer" can be a helpful reminder that we can use our own vulnerability to develop compassion for both ourselves and others. We have been there, so we can relate to that deep sense of loss. At the same time, we have a wealth of perspective that we can draw from, which allows us to have hope for the future.

Mariah Fenton Gladis, author of *Tales Of A Wounded Healer*, is a long-term survivor of ALS (also known as Lou Gehrig's Disease). Mariah understands that life's challenges arrive in many different forms: physical, emotional, and spiritual. She has an amazing ability to use her own personal struggle to deepen her compassion for others' pain, enabling them to heal and move forward with their lives.

Try this:
Go inside and take a deep breath, then let it go. Allow yourself to get in touch with those moments when you rose to the occasion, facing whatever adversity you were confronted with. Acknowledge the strengths you possessed in that moment, which helped you move through it. Use this insight to remind yourself whenever you're having a hard time: you have the inner strengths to draw on that can help you deal with adversity.

If we are willing through meditation to be mindful not only of what feels comfortable, but also of what pain feels like, if we even aspire to stay awake and open to what we're feeling, to recognize and acknowledge it as best we can in each moment, then something begins to change.

—Pema Chödrön

CHAPTER 5

FREE YOUR MIND!

CUT THROUGH YOUR OBSESSIONS

Mad *is a term we use to describe a man who is obsessed with one idea, and nothing else.*

—Ugo Betti

Many people have the common experience of obsessive thinking: we find ourselves going over and over again what we would like to have said to our boss or an irritating co-worker; we can't let go of an argument we had with our spouse; or we're anxious about an exam, a deadline, or how we're going to pay our bills! Yet obsessing over it just wears us out, interferes with sleep, and doesn't really contribute much to solving the problem. In this chapter, we'll look at various ways to shift your mood when you're caught in the vortex of obsessive thoughts.

Four Ways to Free Yourself from Obsessive Thinking

Because we fail to notice that we fail to notice, there is little we can do to change until we notice how failing to notice shapes our thoughts and deeds.

—R. D. Laing

Obsessions can rule our thinking unless we notice that we're caught. Yet trying to escape from our obsession creates a paradox: the harder you try not to think about whatever is bothering you, the more you keep thinking about it. (Try hard not to think about a pink elephant!) So we get caught in a vortex that's really difficult to get out of. Shifting your mood in such circumstances is easier said than done. But, there are a number of strategies that can be helpful!

I. One approach is to simply give in to it: realize you're caught in it, don't try to extricate yourself, but purposely go into the very topic that's obsessing you:

1. Write about it: what's the problem, what do you want, what's getting in the way? Is there anything you can do about it right now? What's the next step you could take to make a difference?

2. Reach out for support to talk about it with a friend, therapist, or sponsor. It can be a great relief to express what's bothering you. It can also help you get a fresh perspective about what you want to do next.

3. Set aside a specific amount of time to obsess about it on purpose: like ten minutes before an appointment when

you know you'll have to get up and focus on something else. By confronting it head on, doing it on purpose, yet limiting the time, it often loses some of its tenacity.

II. Another strategy is to distract yourself by "changing the subject" and directing your attention elsewhere:

1. Watch a movie.
2. Read a book.
3. Get together with a friend for some focused activity (not just talking about your obsession!).
4. Engage in some strenuous exercise.

III. The third approach is to simply become mindful of the obsession, without getting carried away by the content: Ah yes, here's that old obsession again. Like a jingle you can't get out of your head, playing in the background, you don't need to take it all that seriously. When you stop trying so hard to get rid of it or make it stop, it eventually plays itself out.

IV. And the fourth strategy is to shift your mood with **FIRE** Wisdom:

1. **Feel** how the emotional tension shows up in your body.
2. **Intensify** the physical sensation, and hold your breath for a moment.
3. **Release** the tension
4. **Explore** your preference: whether you'd rather feel uptight, or relaxed?

And now, become aware of your own internal wisdom:

What do you know now, from this more relaxed place, about whatever was bothering you? How would you like to handle whatever situation you are faced with?

These strategies can help you realize over time (and with a lot of practice!) that you have a choice about which neural circuitry you want to activate. In other words, would you rather be caught in the grip of your obsession, or relax?

In your everyday life, you can also notice once in a while where your mind is going. If a recent obsession keeps popping up, you can think of your obsession as a train pulling into the station, with a big sign on the front for its destination: self-judgment, recrimination, worry, or shame—whatever the content is of your current obsession. Then you can decide whether you really want to hop on that train of thought, or let it go.

Or driving down the highway, you see an off-ramp for obsession. There's a moment of choice: Do you really want to go down that road? Why get sidetracked by this particular fixation? You realize it usually leads to a dead-end, so let's just pass it by.

In the beginning, you may feel as though you don't really have much choice: it's more like you've been *hijacked!* You find yourself on that train of thought, or sidetracked for an extended period of time before you even notice you're no longer at the train station, or on the main highway.

That's all right, just bring yourself back to your breath. Try gently labeling each obsession as it arises: worry, annoyance, recrimination. This will help you develop your sense of choice: Ah yes, I think I'll let that train go by. Or: Let's not go down that road. I've been there plenty of other times, and that's not where I need to go right now.

Try this:

Go inside for a moment, take a deep breath, then let it go. Imagine that you're on a train platform, and you see a train pulling into the station. On the front of the train is a big sign that says, "Your Current Obsession." Rather than immediately hopping on that train of thought, just imagine letting that train go by.

Here's another example:

Go inside for a moment, take a deep breath, then let it go. Imagine that you're driving down the freeway, and you see an off-ramp with a big sign that says, "Your Current Obsession." Rather than immediately taking that exit, just imagine passing it by. You've been down that road many times before, and you don't need to get side-tracked again.

We needn't be slaves to every association that pops into mind. We don't have to hop on every train of thought that pulls into the station, or go down that road every time we pass a distracting off-ramp along the highway. By maintaining a gentle awareness as they go by, we develop our capacity to generate new pathways of harmony, ease, and joy.

Three Natural Cures for Insomnia

O sleep, O gentle sleep,
Nature's soft nurse, how have I frightened thee,
That thou no more wilt weigh my eye-lids down
And steep my senses in forgetfulness?
—Shakespeare, Henry IV

Most people have at least occasional trouble falling asleep at night, especially when they're worried about something, so they keep going over it in their minds, hoping to solve it or reach some resolution, but the relief of sleep eludes them as they toss and turn.

The trouble with using sleeping pills on a consistent basis is that they generally do not provide the full range of deep sleep and dreaming that we need to restore ourselves. Drug-based sleep aids can rapidly lose their effectiveness, with a rebound affect that makes it more difficult to fall asleep on your own, so it's easy to become dependent on them.

Here are three natural, non-drug strategies for getting a better night's sleep, even in the face of obsession:

1. After tossing and turning and continuing to dwell on your obsession, you can try giving up. Just get up, and write about it (using the steps mentioned above), until you feel tired.

2. Get up and do something else to distract you, like reading a book (no murder mysteries!), or even some mundane chore like cleaning the bathroom. I know some people can fall asleep watching TV, but it's usually not a great idea, because you can get caught up in the story, and the light can interfere with getting drowsy again.

3. Try this counting exercise:

Count your breaths, alternating backwards and forwards, from one to ten: one, ten; two, nine; three, eight; and so on.

The advantage of this method is that it gives your mind something else to do (a distraction), that takes a certain amount of attention and effort, but it's fairly boring and meaningless, so eventually your mind pulls away from it, and your natural sleepiness can kick in.

If one to ten is too easy, try alternating backwards and forwards from one to a hundred with each breath: 1, 100; 2, 99; 3, 98; etc.

The purpose of all these approaches is to release our minds from the vortex they sometimes get sucked into! Obsession is merely another example of getting hijacked by our moods. But over time, as we develop newer pathways, we gain a greater freedom from obsession, as we cultivate the more relaxed source of our own wisdom.

It's also helpful to develop better sleep habits, such as avoiding excessive caffeine and alcohol, stop looking at blue-light devices well before bedtime, get some exercise during the day, and keep a regular bedtime schedule.

The Dog-Walker Who Couldn't Stop Checking

Molly worked as a dog-walker for up to six families at a time. But her job was in jeopardy because whenever she dropped off a dog, she kept going back to check the door to make sure it was really locked. She'd go back as many as ten times to make certain that the dog couldn't get out. She was afraid the owners might come home to find their door unlocked and their dog gone. But she kept falling behind on her schedule, not returning some dogs until the owner was already home, wondering where their dog was!

She also checked her stove over and over again, so it was hard to leave the house for fear the house would burn down; although it was slightly easier for her to believe that she had locked her own door when she left in the morning.

I wanted to get a clear picture of her experience and her beliefs at the moment she dropped off her dogs. "I'm sure I locked the door," she said. "I keep checking it to make sure it's locked, but when I walk away, I become filled with doubt, and I can't keep myself from going back to check it again."

I asked her go inside for a moment, and imagine she was at the doorstep of one of her clients. "You've just dropped off the dog, let it inside, closed the door, and locked it. Then you check it again to make sure it's locked. What are you experiencing now?"

"I feel pretty good; I'm sure it's locked."

"Now step away from the door, and tell me what you're experiencing, physically."

"I get tense in my shoulders, and I feel this pressure, like I have to move, I have go and check it again."

"So imagine yourself going back to check it again. How does that feel?"

"Much better."

I said "I'd like to try an experiment. Let's go out in the hallway, and I'll give you the key to lock my office door. I'll stand next to you while you lock it, and after you check it, I'll check it, too, to make sure it's locked."

So we went out to the hallway, I gave her my key, and she locked the door. "Is it locked?" I asked.

"Yes. It's definitely locked."

I tried the door. "Yup, it seems totally locked to me, too. How do you feel, just standing here next to the locked door?"

"I feel pretty calm. I know it's locked."

"All right. So why don't you walk down the hall, and just feel what happens inside your body while you're walking away from the door."

Molly started walking briskly and confidently at first, but then she slowed down, and I could see her hunch her shoulders. "What are you experiencing right now?"

"I feel really anxious, like I have to go back and check the door."

I said "Just stay for a moment with your physical sensations. Where in your body do you feel this compulsion to go back and check?"

She closed her eyes and went inside. "My shoulders are really tense. I feel like my arm wants to reach out to check the door."

"Go ahead and reach out your arm, as if you were checking the door."

She tried that, but it just made her more anxious.

"Do you remember, just a moment ago, you were sure it was locked. And I checked it, too, so I'm certain it's locked. See, I'm pressing on the handle, and it doesn't budge."

She looked hesitant.

"You don't really believe me, huh?"

She shook her head. "No, I would have to check it myself."

"Sure, that's fine; come on back, and we'll try it again."

So she came back to the door, and checked it.

"Is it locked?" I asked.

She nodded.

"Are you sure?"

"I'm pretty sure."

"Why don't you check it again."

She checked it again, and said "It's definitely locked."

So at that point, instead of sending her down the hall, I suggested "Go inside, and feel the certainty of that door being locked, right now, standing next to it, after you've just checked it. Go ahead and put your hand on it, and feel the solidness of the door handle. It doesn't budge, right?"

She nodded.

"You're totally sure the door is locked, and now allow yourself to feel that certainty in the very core of your body, feel the certainty of that locked door."

"Yes I feel it."

"Now open your eyes, and try walking down the hall again, holding this certainty as you go."

This time she got considerably farther before she lost her confidence that the door was locked.

We tried this exercise a number of times over the next several weeks, and she gradually became more confident that she had indeed locked the door, without feeling a compulsive need to check it again.

But the real challenge to her increasing confidence was whether she could put this new-found ability into practice when she dropped off her dogs.

She had some good days and some bad days. On the worst days, she was back to her previous pattern of returning up to ten times to check the lock.

At one point I suggested that instead of fighting it, she could even try checking the lock twenty times. This was comforting to her, but it didn't have the hoped-for paradoxical effect: by repeatedly checking it even many more times than she really "needed" to, I was hoping she could feel less anxious. And that she might even get bored with the assignment, since by that time she'd already be certain it was locked!

I think this strategy may have helped, but I don't think it was as effective as simply having her pay closer attention not only to what she was actually doing when she locked the door, but also how she felt inside. I was hoping she could register a greater awareness of locking the door, plus her own internal *certainty* that it was locked.

On the good days, she could get away after only checking the door two or three times, certainly within the range of not really interfering with her job. She also made considerable progress at home on her compulsion to check her stove to make sure it was off. Since it was a gas stove, she could see that the flame was out. She could also place her hand over the burner, so she could tell that it wasn't hot. There was no smell of gas, and she couldn't hear the hiss. As she increased her mindfulness of turning off the stove, she could check the flame, feel the lack of heat, and notice how it felt, physically, to be certain the stove was off. This sequence of becoming mindful of both her actions and all her senses provided her some relief from her stove-checking.

Molly's story, of course, is simply a more tenacious example of the need many of us have at times to check the door to make sure we locked it. We tend to second-guess ourselves when we don't pay close enough attention to whatever we're doing.

I believe the source of our unease about whether we've really accomplished a task is that we commonly perform many common activities "mindlessly" on automatic, without being aware of what we're actually doing, so it doesn't really register in our bodies. We lack the internal, physical certainty that could reinforce our memory. By becoming more mindful of what we're doing in any given moment, we're much more likely to believe that we've already completed a given task.

So it wasn't simply a matter of trying to convince Molly that she had locked the door. She needed a *gut experience* of her *recognition* that she had locked the door. So she trained herself over a number of sessions (and through hundreds of dog-walks) to take a moment to really register the completion of her task on a physical level.

Romantic Obsession

If you have it [Love], you don't need to have anything else, and if you don't have it, it doesn't matter much what else you have.

—James M. Barrie

Love obsessions, even though they have a romantic tinge to them, can be very painful. I certainly can vouch for that from my own experience: in my youth, I frequently found myself yearning for someone who barely realized I existed! And yet in some ways I was addicted to longing. There's a tormented, romantic sweetness about longing, a poignant but illusory hope that someday the object of my affection will come to their senses and see that *I'm the one they've been waiting for!* In the meantime, I can bask in my tormented fantasy, without having to deal with the joys and challenges of dealing with a real relationship.

Debbie came to my office, determined to get her boyfriend Todd to marry her—the only trouble was, he was already married!

But she was convinced that his marriage was a sham and he was really in love with *her*. She claimed his wife treated him badly, they never slept together anymore, and that he was just too weak-willed to divorce her. In the meantime, they spent a great deal of time together, since they worked in the same office, and Debbie didn't care who noticed her flirting with him. She came into therapy wanting suggestions about how to convince him to leave his wife.

I asked if she'd ever seen the movie, My *Best Friend's Wedding*, about a woman named Jules who becomes obsessed with Michael, her former boyfriend, once he's about to marry his fiancee, Kimmy. At one point, Kimmy discovers Jules trying to kiss Michael, and she runs off, devastated by his apparent betrayal. Michael pulls away from Jules, and runs after Kimmy, who jumps in her car and speeds away with Michael in hot pursuit. Jules steals a van to chase Michael. As she's careening through traffic she calls her gay friend George, who had encouraged her to tell Michael how she felt, and asks what she should do as she races after him. He says, "You were kissing him; was he kissing you?"

"Well that's when Kimmy caught us, and he ran off."

"He's chasing her, and you're chasing him. The question is, 'Who's chasing *you?*'"

Debbie stared at me disdainfully. "Yes," she said, icily. "A number of people have suggested I watch that movie." I also asked if she'd heard of the book *He's Just Not That Into You*, by Greg Behrendt and Liz Tuccillo, who had worked with the TV series *Sex in the City*. She was not amused.

I thought we might make some headway after it finally dawned on her that despite the occasional furtive encounter, Todd really wasn't available. He married Barbara, after all, not Debbie; even though he and Debbie had been friends for years before he got married.

After our first session, she called to say she didn't think we were a good match, and never came back.

I bring up this unfortunate example simply to show the delusional aspect of romantic obsession. I admit there may have been a more skillful and less confrontational approach to her situation. I didn't think it was ethical to help her break up Todd's marriage, although I was willing to help her get over her obsession with a man who was obviously unavailable. But Debbie wanted validation for her goal, not assistance in getting over it; in fact, her entire aim was to *get her man!* And if I wouldn't help her, she'd find someone else who would.

I think that part of the tenacity of romantic obsession is that it's a very powerful form of denial, that's reinforced by our attachment to a certain outcome. Even though that outcome is essentially delusional, it's fueled by a rush of *dopamine* when we're initially infatuated with someone. In normal romantic relationships, that fire cools somewhat as we get to know the other person and *oxytocin* kicks in, with its warm feeling of loving affection. But when there's an obstacle in the way, our obsession is never satisfied, so we keep burning with desire! We become convinced that the object of our craving is our *only* source of happiness, so we hold on to our misery as though it were a lifeboat, little realizing it's sinking us like an anchor.

So, how to chill?

One way of course is to get a straight answer from the other person: are they really interested in us? That's difficult to do if we're getting mixed messages; maybe they don't even know their own minds! Even if they're not really available, they're obviously getting something out of leading us on.

So then we need to look at their *behavior:* do they call when they say they will? Do they initiate contact? Do they seem glad to see us? Do they treat us well? If we have a disagreement, are they willing to talk about it and work something out? Do they acknowledge any practical obstacles, and are they willing to work on them?

I had another client named Alice, who was hung up on Tony, a soldier she'd had a brief affair with when they were in the service. After they were both discharged, he moved to Los Angeles and was living with his mother. Alice met his mother once, and was convinced his mother hated her: she was poisoning Tony's mind against her, and that was the only reason they couldn't be together.

But after a while, she began to realize that Tony wasn't available—he had moved to L.A., after all—and it sank in that despite their romantic fling, he wasn't moving back any time soon. He kept her hanging on by telling her he wanted to see her, it's just that the timing wasn't right.

So eventually, she was able to feel into the truth of his unavailability: he's in L.A., not here, and doesn't seem to be doing much to move back, invite her to visit, come see her, or even return her phone calls.

This gut-wrenching realization was hard to accept, but she finally was able to. It's a more challenging use of mindfulness, because when I had her go inside, what she was most in touch with was her intense desire, which seemed much more "true" and real, than the doubts that kept gnawing at her (and which in fact, brought her into therapy in the first place).

She could feel the tension in her longing. But when she cranked it up and then relaxed, she knew in her heart, despite the mixed messages, that he wasn't coming back. Romantic obsession can be understood as a defense against grief: acknowledging the truth of the absence (or loss) of love. She still wanted to blame his mother, but the truth is, *no man is going to let his mother get in the way of being with the woman he truly loves.*

Intrusive Memories—and a Missing Experience

My mother was born in New Braunfels, Texas, which had been settled by German immigrants in the 1840s. She spoke German before she learned English in school. She and her mother spent her early years on her grandparents' farm, where she earned fifty cents a day picking cotton. In the 1920s, they had a cistern that collected rain water, and they used a hand pump to fill a big wash-basin to boil their clothes. They used kerosene lanterns, and during the winter, they heated irons on the wood stove to warm up their beds.

Her great-grandmother lived in the attic, and pretended to be an invalid. But during the day, when the other adults were out in the fields, she'd go through the house and snoop through everyone's drawers. She gave my mom dried lemon peels she had hidden away in her sewing box to chew on.

While I was growing up, in addition to these other tales, my mother would sometimes tell us how badly her mother treated her: she told her she was ugly, and that no man would ever want to marry her. This was quite absurd, as my mother was a great beauty, and incredibly engaging! (I know many sons have a soft spot in their hearts for their mom, but I'm not the only one who thought so.)

Her mother sent her to a Catholic school in Texas while her mom pursued a romance in Los Angeles. Whenever she giggled in class (which apparently she did a lot), those "mean nuns" told her to stick out her hands so they could whack them with a ruler. They made her kneel in penance on splintered boards for hours at a time, until she got boils on her knees.

After six months, she pleaded with her mother to let her come home. Her mother finally let her come live with her again after her latest affair ended. It was in the midst of the Great Depression, and my mom sold candy bars on the streets of Los Angeles to help support them. When she turned eighteen, her mother told her she was quitting her job, because now it was my mom's turn to support *her*.

She had the gumption to tell her mother she needed to live her own life. She got a job in a boarding house and put herself through college. She found out later that her mother had tried to undermine her position by telling her boss that she was really Jewish, because her father was a Jew (even though he wasn't). Fortunately, her boss wasn't anti-Semitic, and simply ignored her mother's ravings.

After college, my mom joined the Marine Corps, where she met my father. They got married during World War II. Despite previous conflicts with her mother, Mom allowed her to move in with us when she was dying of cancer. My grandmother was frail, and mostly bed-ridden. Yet even then, I remember her telling me that my mother never really loved me. I didn't believe her, and thought she was delusional. But I had a glimpse of what my mother must have experienced growing up with her.

Later in life, Mom has lost some of her short-term memory. Nonetheless, she has quite a sense of humor, and we often tease each other. She's still a "giggle box" (those "mean nuns" couldn't beat it out of her!), and she even jokes about her own memory loss. "My forgetter is better than my rememberer," she likes to say. Once she asked me, "Have you ever known anyone whose forgetter is better than mine?"

"I gotta admit, you take the cake!"

"Well, I don't like to brag," she said. Then we both cracked up.

Yet every once in a while, she seems to get trapped in memories of her mother treating her badly. A few years ago, whenever it came up in conversation, it didn't seem all that different from previous stories, and we'd just naturally move on to other topics. Over time, it's become more difficult for her to shift her attention, once she gets stuck in these painful memories. Then she gets increasingly agitated, which is common among older people with short-term memory loss.

When that happens, dementia experts suggest changing the subject, so our loved ones can stop dwelling on the same topic. I don't want to seem rude or uncaring about what she's been through, yet I realize there may be times when she's unable to pull herself out of it.

When she starts down that road, I tend to get drawn in, myself. It's a fine line between acknowledging her memories, yet not getting stuck there. After a while, I'll see if we can shift our attention to the hummingbird hovering at the feeder outside the window. "Look at that one, with its shiny red throat." Or I'll suggest we go outside, to see what those rascally rabbits are up to in her garden! Getting up and moving to another location seems to help. Something as simple as "Let's go fix some lunch!" interrupts the usual cycle. Once she's engaged with another activity, the storm passes, and she seems fine again.

One time, remembering her childhood in Texas before moving to L.A., she said her mother complained about getting stuck with such an ugly child. "How could anyone ever tell you, 'You're an ugly child'?" she asked.

I hesitated for a moment, not sure if we should keep talking about it. But I was struck by how painful that must have been, to have her own mother treat her that way! So I said, "Yeah, how could she talk trash like that! You were such a sweet and adorable little girl."

"Darn tootin'!" she said, and clunked the table with her fist.

Just at that moment, the song "How Could Anyone" by Libby Roderick came to mind. So I took her hand, and sang her this song (see below).*

She seemed transfixed, and suddenly all the mean things her mother did and said about her drifted away. For some time afterwards, she just basked in the glow of our loving moment together.

    * Libby kindly gave me permission to make a video singing "How Could Anyone" for my mom: go to my channel at www.youtube.com/ShiftYourMood and click on Shift Your Mood—How Could Anyone.

CHAPTER 6

SELF-SOOTHING

CALM YOUR INNER GUARD DOG

I wish I could show you when you are lonely or in darkness the astonishing light of your own being.

—Hafiz

We've been talking so far about our response to external circumstances, but I think our greatest opportunity for self-soothing is becoming friendlier with ourselves!

So many people get down on themselves for the simplest mistakes, with a barrage of harsh criticism: How could you be so stupid, what an idiot, and so on. I suspect many of us have internalized the verbal abuse of parents, teachers, and even school-yard bullies.

You can think of this inner critic as a harsher version of your Guard Dog: trying to keep you in line, rein you in, or make you behave in some acceptable fashion. The positive intent is a protective function; the problem is that it comes across in such a punitive manner. Instead of encouraging us, it tends to shame us, lowering our self-esteem, which makes it even less likely that we'll be able to follow through on our best intentions.

Seven Steps to Calm Your Guard Dog and Tame Your Inner Critic

Here's a systematic method to calm your Guard Dog and tame that inner critic:

1. Recognize the critic: (like, "You stupid idiot!")
—Oh, here I am harshly condemning myself.

2. What's the protective function of the Guard Dog?
—Wanting to do a good job.

3. What's the irrational belief?
—That I should always be perfect, and never make a mistake.

4. Get in touch with the underlying feeling:
—I'm disappointed I made that mistake.

5. Feel how this emotion registers in your body:
—I feel constricted, and pulled in.

6. Tighten the constriction, hold your breath, then let it go.

7. From this more relaxed place, get in touch with a more realistic view of your true abilities:
—Yes I messed up, and I'm disappointed with myself, but I've learned something from this mistake, and I can use that insight to do better next time.

When I've clunked my head against the cupboard door for the umpteenth time, I still get mad at myself, even after all these years! But it doesn't last as long. After the first rush of annoyance, I can catch myself fairly quickly now, and instead of continuing to condemn myself, I try having more compassion: "Oh, poor guy, that really hurts! Yes, another painful reminder to watch where I'm going, slow down, pay more attention to what I'm doing." Then I put a cold pack on my head, and relax for a while before going back to work.

Panic Attacks

Julio came to see me because he was suffering from panic attacks during his exams for some very challenging classes in advanced calculus and physics. He said he knew the material very well, and had already been accepted to U.C. Berkeley for grad school. But his acceptance was contingent on his final grades.

At first, he thought there was something physically wrong with him: his heart started beating very fast and he began to sweat. Breathing faster, he felt waves of nausea and dizziness. He even went to the emergency room, thinking he might be dying of heart failure, but they could find nothing wrong with him. They told him he was having a panic attack.

I said it was great that he got checked out to make sure there was nothing wrong with him physically. I assured him that even though his symptoms were incredibly unpleasant, he wasn't going to die from having a panic attack.

Knowing this fact can help panic attacks seem more manageable. One of the ways they perpetuate themselves is through the belief that something is terribly wrong. You get an adrenalin rush in response to this belief, which activates all of your fight or flight responses. Your heart starts pounding, and you begin to sweat. Your mind then interprets this as more evidence of danger, which scares you even more, and you get another jolt of adrenalin. Breathing quickly can lead to hyperventilating, which can cause tingling and numb sensations (and even cramping) in your hands and feet.

Julio had also experienced some of these attacks while getting together with friends, or going out for a drink. It turned out that alcohol, which he was essentially using to self-medicate, seemed to exacerbate his tendency to get panicky when he was out with his friends. He would cover it up by saying he didn't feel well and needed to go home. As we were discussing his history, Julio also made a link between drinking the night before, and feeling panicky during class the next day, especially if there was an exam.

Julio would often rather stay home than risk having a panic attack when he went out, which is a common strategy. Many people who suffer panic attacks become *agoraphobic*, which means "fear of the marketplace." They feel safer at home, and less anxious when they don't go out, so it becomes self-reinforcing to stay at home and thus avoid risking another attack. These attacks were definitely interfering with both his social life and his academic career.

I asked him if the doctor at the emergency room had recommended any medication, since anti-depressants and anti-anxiety agents are sometimes prescribed for panic attacks. He said he'd rather try to handle it on his own, and not use any medication.

Relaxation Exercise

It's difficult to be relaxed and anxious at the same time, so we started out with a simple systematic relaxation exercise.

We may not even realize where we're holding tension in our body. With this exercise, we'll go through each part of your body, tense it for a moment, take in a deep breath, hold it, then relax and let it go.

Take in a deep breath and tense your feet. Hold your breath for a moment, then let it go and relax your feet.

Take in a deep breath and tense your calf muscles. Hold your breath for a moment, then let it go and relax your calves.

Take in a deep breath and tense your thighs. Hold your breath for a moment, then let it go and relax your thighs.

Take in a deep breath and tense your buttocks. Hold your breath for a moment, then let it go and relax your buttocks.

Take in a deep breath and tense your stomach. Hold your breath for a moment, then let it go and relax your stomach.

Take in a deep breath and tense your back. Hold your breath for a moment, then let it go and relax your back.

Take in a deep breath and tense your chest. Hold your breath for a moment, then let it go and relax your chest.

Take in a deep breath and make a fist with each hand. Hold your breath for a moment, then let it go and relax your hands.

Take in a deep breath and make a muscle with your biceps. (I think of this as the Super Hero pose!) Hold your breath for a moment, then let it go and relax your arms.

Take in a deep breath and shrug your shoulders. Hold your breath for a moment, then let it go and relax your shoulders.

Take in a deep breath and scrunch up your face. Hold your breath for a moment, then let it go and relax your face.

After doing this exercise, I often feel much more relaxed than when I first started out. Increasing the tension in each part of your body helps you relax it even more. It works on a similar principle we've tried previously to shift your mood: only this time you initiate the constriction in each part of your body, hold your breath for a moment, and then release.

Which brings us to the next technique: shifting your attention. Instead of getting caught up in this cascade of panicky thoughts about "something terrible is happening to me," it helps to remember that nothing is really wrong with you, so you don't need to panic!

What I find especially useful about mindfulness, is that it increases our ability to step out off the train of thoughts that add to the panic. You can then reassure yourself you're not going to die: "Oh, here I am having panic symptoms, but there isn't really anything wrong with me. Because I'm already activated, my heart's going to beat wildly for a few minutes, so it's going to take a while before all of my alarm systems subside. In the meantime, let's try to relax and breathe normally."

In Julio's example, he'd come to class all prepared to take his exam, then he'd come across a problem that required extra concentration to solve it. But instead of systematic-ally solving the problem, he would get caught in the vortex of a panicky thought: "What if I can't solve this problem? I'll flunk this test and never get into Berkeley!" Then he'd get incredibly frustrated with himself: "Stop being such an idiot! What's your problem? *Just concentrate!*"

At which point the whole cascade of panic symptoms would ensue: his heart pounding, breathing hard, his hands getting sweaty, and feeling nauseated. Under those circum-stances, it's really difficult for anyone to concentrate, no matter how smart you are!

So we practiced having him catch himself at the point where he was about to make that leap. Instead of panicking that he might not be able to solve this problem (then flunk the test, flunk the class, and never get into Cal), he was able to mark it and go on to the next problem. He'd remind himself that he really does know his material, he just needs to soothe himself until he feels calmer, and then he'll be able to focus again.

If he got stuck, instead of condemning himself, which only made his symptoms worse, he tried to recognize his own activation: "Oh, I'm in a flight or fight response, which makes it difficult to focus and think. Now let's slow down, and just feel where I'm getting uptight in my body: crank it up, hold my breath, and let it go. Now we can systematically examine all the steps it takes to solve each problem."

This method, of course, could only work because he had practiced it before the test, and because he had done his homework. Relaxing is no panacea; you obviously can't expect to take an exam successfully if you haven't prepared for it! Yet if you know the material, and it's simply anxiety that's getting in the way, you can shift from worrying about the outcome (or condemning yourself), and bring your attention to the actual problem in front of you.

This is also a helpful technique with public speaking. Instead of putting all your attention on yourself, how you're coming across, whether you're making any sense, or how your audience might be judging you, shift your focus to what you'd like your audience to understand about what you're trying to say. This takes your attention off yourself and the quality of your performance, and shifts it to the content of your material. Or in Julio's case, he takes the focus off his worries about whether he'll get into grad school, and shifts to the problem that's actually in front of him on the exam.

At one point, when Julio was feeling discouraged, I suggested going inside to get in touch with his larger goal: what did he want to accomplish by getting an advanced degree in engineering?

He was dedicated to developing alternative energy, so I suggested he imagine how satisfying it would feel one day to be working on a sustainable energy project. A slight smile appeared on his face, as he got in touch again with the reason why he was working so hard in the first place.

I said "Really feel into the pleasure of your vision: how glad you are, right now, about how wonderful it will feel to be working on these projects. Savor the sense of accomplishment and contribution you'll be making. Feel it in the very core of your body: in your heart, and in the pleasure of the smile on your face, just thinking about it. And realize that this confidence, encouragement, and vision is a resource you can always tap into." He smiled, and nodded.

Then, as he felt in touch with this clear vision, I asked him what he could tell that part of himself that gets uptight and anxious about his exams.

"I'm perfectly capable of solving these problems. I know the material, and I have a clear vision of why I'm working so hard in the first place: to develop sustainable energy. So right now, let's just relax, pay attention to the exam, and take one problem at a time."

Developing Self-Love

To love oneself is the beginning of a life-long romance.

—Oscar Wilde

You often hear people say "You can't love anyone else unless you can love yourself." And there may be some truth to that, but I also think this assumption can be unnecessarily harsh and self-blaming, especially for those who have felt abused, abandoned, and bereft of love. For how are we ever able to love ourselves, unless we have felt loved by others?

If we're lucky, we grow up in families who genuinely love us, and that love resonates within our hearts and allows us to grow according to our true nature. But many of us are not that fortunate: emotional, physical, and sexual abuse all take their toll. Many parents are so preoccupied with their own pain that they're not available to witness and nurture their children's emotional lives. Or there may have been so many miss-steps along the way that we're left confused and mistrustful even of ourselves, much less others. But the longing is still there, to have that loving connection that all of us crave.

When we are hurt (as we inevitably are), we have the capacity to heal. Yet repetitive wounds can lead us to protect ourselves. Part of that protection is a kind of insularity, shutting ourselves off from others. Then it's difficult to trust our own natural capacity to heal, grow, and love. Our own suspicion can elicit fear from others as our guard dogs snap and snarl at each other like wounded animals, caught in a vicious circle of punitive reactions and painful retribution.

Let's not take each others' fear and pain so personally! Their negative reactions to their own pain may be directed toward us, but they usually have little to do with us; not that we're always innocent bystanders, since it's easy to get caught in a cycle of mutual retaliation. But if we become aware of our own capacity for fellow-feeling, we can empathize with the pain, even if we still need to protect ourselves from abusive behavior.

We don't have to be totally self-actualized to have a relationship, and in fact relationships of many kinds can go a long way toward healing our previous wounds and repairing our damaged sense of being all right in the world. Human contact can actually provide us with some of the loving experiences we've missed out on, and this can help us generate emotional well-being.

Instead of assuming you have to love yourself before you can love anyone else, I suspect it may work better the other way around: *by loving others, we come to be more in love with ourselves,* and less grasping. Because we're less needy, we feel more fulfilled: we're all right, full of love, just the way we are.

Loving Presence

The most precious gift we can offer others is our presence. When mindfulness embraces those we love, they will bloom like flowers.

—Thich Nhat Hanh

Loving presence is the ability to be present in a loving and empathic way, not demanding anything from the other person, just being present. Carl Rogers described this compassionate presence as "unconditional positive regard," expressed through "warmth, empathy, and genuineness"— caring deeply, feeling an emotional connection with another person, and being who you really are—without pretense or hidden agendas. Thomas Lewis, in his book *A*

General Theory of Love, calls this compassionate connection *limbic resonance*, because it activates the limbic system in the brain.

In my work with couples, when they truly empathize with one another, their mutual compassion creates an incredible opening. Conflicts that previously seemed like irreconcilable differences suddenly become far more manageable. Even if there are still problems to solve, an opening occurs. Where previously there had been suspicion and mistrust, there is now renewed hope and cautious optimism.

Try this:

Make eye contact with someone while feeling your own loving presence. You don't have to say anything, just look, and enjoy each other's presence.

If you have a partner, gaze into each other's eyes for a few moments, and notice what this elicits: memories, images, or sensations? Fear, insecurity, or doubt? Longing, arousal, or a loving connection?

Try it in public. You don't necessarily need someone else's awareness of what you're up to. See what happens when you look upon each person you meet with loving presence: at work, with friends and family members, or even waiting in line at the grocery store. You might try seeing each person as Jesus or Buddha, Mary or Quan Yin (the Bodhisattva of compassion), a loving spirit, or simply a fellow human being (whatever metaphor works for you!), and see how it shifts your own perception and internal feelings.

When you make eye contact, you're looking through a window into the "soul" or present awareness of another conscious being. We can at least acknowledge to ourselves (even if it seems too weird to say it out loud), "I see you in there, peering out at me."

Loving presence often emerges with eye contact, or the simple expression of affection—on the shoulder, holding your hand, stroking your hair, or a warm embrace—and it can fill you with an abiding friendliness, connection, and well-being.

How can we be engaged, without clinging? Allow the other person to be who they are, without excessive demands that they gratify us in a particular way. Allow yourself to feel a natural curiosity about this being in front of you: what's it like to be looking out at the world through their eyes?

Try this out when you're with another person:

Notice when you feel connected, and how you allow yourself to be present. What shifts in your body? Relax into it.

When you feel yourself drawn to someone, what comes up for you? Whatever you admire about the other person is a seed within you.

Likewise, notice when you feel yourself pulling away, without a lot of judgment and noise, worrying about how "neurotic" you are. Just feel the constriction with curiosity: oh, here's a situation where I find myself pulling back. What happens in my body that allows me to gauge the amount of contact I'm comfortable with? These are clues that can allow us to assess real danger, versus a more conditioned pulling away.

Test it out: feel the tension, and see what happens if you make yourself even more tense. What if you allowed yourself to relax? Take in a deep breath, let it go, and feel how that affects your emotional state. Look away, and then look back again. Check in with your breathing, your heartbeat, feel the moisture or dryness in your hands, in your mouth, in your eyes.

True solace, acceptance, and love arise from deeply-felt empathy, expressed through loving kindness and compassion.

CHAPTER 7

BOOST YOUR HAPPINESS QUOTIENT!

RAISE YOUR SET-POINT OF HAPPINESS

The basic root of happiness lies in our minds; outer circumstances are nothing more than adverse or favorable.
—Matthieu Ricard

The Paradox of Seeking Happiness

The obsessive pursuit of pleasure is like chasing a rainbow: the faster we run, the more it recedes. Instead of simply enjoying the rainbow, we end up experiencing our own grasping.

Recent studies selected Denmark as the happiest country in the world (the U.S. ranked twenty-third). Researchers speculate that Danes have rather modest expectations about what's really possible. They also have free health care and education, plus generous parental leave, and six weeks of paid vacation a year! They have one of the lowest income gaps in the world, which encourages a more egalitarian society with shared communal ties and interests.

They're not greatly distressed when things don't go as well as they wished, since they don't usually have overblown expectations to begin with. As a culture, Danes appear to be somewhat reserved; so I wondered how they expressed their sense of well-being. I asked a Danish man I met recently about this study. He was a little embarrassed to be put on the spot, as if he could represent all Danes, or that he should exemplify Danish happiness. He said even though his country rates high on the happiness scale, they're not all skipping down the street to express their constant joy. When asked how things are going, a common expression is "Det kunne være værre" (it could be worse). There may be something to be said for avoiding unrealistic expectations! Yet overall, he agreed that many Danes seem to be fairly content with their lives.

Danes have a special word for this experience of contentment and well-being, called *hygge*, which means a cozy sense of familiar trust and togetherness, with an ease of social flow and camaraderie among family and loved ones.

We have a tendency in American culture to assume that fame, fortune, and the latest gadgets will make us happy, and then we're surprised when they don't. But rather than learning a lesson from that fact, we simply go after something even flashier and more exciting, still supposing the answer must be out there, somewhere.

People often think of happiness in terms of various pleasures: sex, food, or thrilling experiences. All of these can be quite enjoyable, but the pleasure we feel doesn't last very long. Another paradox of happiness is that living a life solely dedicated to seeking one sensual experience after another can easily lead to addictions and compulsive behavior.

While it's true that the lives of people who are destitute can be genuinely improved by better circumstances, for most middle class people whose basic needs for food, housing, and health care are satisfied, a vast increase of wealth is not likely to alter our basic experience of well-being. In his book, *Stumbling on Happiness,* Daniel Gilbert offers an insightful and provocative look at the common mistakes people make when they try to assess their own future happiness. It turns out that we mistakenly believe that we will feel much worse after bad news, and much better following a positive event, than we actually do!

Studies have compared lottery winners, for example, with people who have had terrible accidents that left them paralyzed. Some of those who were paralyzed even considered suicide immediately after the accident, but surprisingly enough, after a year or two, most have usually adapted pretty well to their current limitations.

And lottery winners, even though they experienced an initial period of excitement and elation, weren't necessarily happier a year later. In fact, many were bored and depressed, because they quit their jobs and no longer saw people on a regular basis. Some had spent more money than they had won, and even gone into debt. Others became alienated from friends and family members who felt entitled to share in their winnings.

Instead of looking outside ourselves for major sources of happiness, let's look at some ways to get in touch with our own natural, internal resources that we can use to enhance our sense of purpose, meaning, and contentment.

The Neuroscience of Happiness

Happiness is an inside job.

—Sylvia Boorstein

Positive psychology and the "neuroscience of happiness" counter the usual assumption that seeking pleasure is the key to contentment.

Yet there are ways to enhance our well-being, since we now know a lot more about the essential conditions of happiness. Martin Seligman, in his book *Authentic Happiness*, identifies these as pleasure, engagement, and meaning. He goes on to distinguish the differences between these three: "We call a tendency to pursue happiness by boosting positive emotion, 'the pleasant life'; the tendency to pursue happiness via the gratifications, 'the good life'; and the tendency to pursue happiness via using our strengths towards something larger than ourselves, 'the meaningful life.' A person who uses all three routes to happiness leads the 'full life' and recent empirical evidence suggests that those who lead the full life have much greater life satisfaction."

I would add a fourth aspect to these: serenity or contentment, which arises from being in the present, conscious of your own awareness.

Christopher Peterson, co-author (with Martin Seligman) of *Signature Strengths and Virtues* encourages us to discover and develop our *signature strengths*: those talents and qualities that come to us naturally. Instead of clunking our heads against the wall of our most challenging deficits, we can nurture what we already love to do (and that we're already good at!). We get more immediate rewards and validation, which can help us feel more confident and engaged with the world.

Freud suggested love and work as major sources of fulfillment: intimate connections with a partner, family, and friends, and a meaningful sense of purpose.

In addition, finding and contributing something beyond yourself, by doing something you find inherently interesting and worthwhile—whether through spirituality, politics, or volunteering for a cause you believe in—can also contribute to well-being, engagement, and meaning. Developing some confidence in our abilities can also lead to an experience of *efficacy:* the actions we take can have an effect by making a difference in other people's lives!

Flow

Let the beauty of what you love be what you do.

—Rumi

Being totally involved with an engrossing activity can lead to a satisfying experience of "flow." Mihaly Csikszentmihalyi (pronounced "cheek-sent-me-high-ee") the author of *Flow*, suggests we're in *flow* when we have enough of a challenge to engage us, but not so much that we feel overwhelmed. This provides a wonderful optimization of experience: we find ourselves in a timeless, flowing engagement with whatever we're doing.

Creative activities are prime examples, such as playing music, dancing, writing, or painting. Exercise and sports help us engage in *flow* by releasing endorphins, which are neurotransmitters of pleasure. Making love can be a wonderful experience of flow, especially when you're really in sync with your partner. Whenever you feel fully absorbed with work, you may be experiencing flow. Yet even more receptive, contemplative activities such as meditation, a quiet walk, or gazing at a beautiful landscape can also be lovely ways of cultivating this special quality.

Mindfulness offers another way to experience flow by helping us get in touch with being-in-the-moment, which ends the chase, and can be gratifying in itself: another example of the paradox of happiness! Instead of striving to get somewhere, we find relief by easing into the present moment, and letting go.

Rather than grasping at whatever catches our attention—whether it's the latest gadget, sex, money, or power—we can assess whether a given action really serves us. We can also take a moment to gauge what's at stake for us, even in the face of difficult circumstances. Then we can be more responsive, rather than reactive.

Follow Your Bliss

If you follow your bliss, you put yourself on a kind of track that has been there all the while, waiting for you, and the life that you ought to be living is the one you are living. . . follow your bliss and don't be afraid, and doors will open where you didn't know they were going to be.

—Joseph Campbell

Joseph Campbell, interviewed by Bill Moyers in the documentary series *The Power of Myth*, encourages us to follow our bliss: go after those interests that seem to capture our imagination in a consistent way (similar to Peterson's signature strengths), even if we're not sure they will ever earn us a living or even be appreciated by anyone else. It doesn't matter, because these interests feed our souls. Getting in touch with the natural state of contentment that arises from our true interests can help us live more authentically. Campbell said, "if you are following your bliss, you are enjoying that refreshment, that life within you, all the time."

Following interests that nourish us can provide a nurturing background to our daily lives. When things get hectic, we know that there are some areas of our life that seem uncontaminated by the hustle and bustle of the everyday world. You may recall how Nathaniel re-discovered the joy he felt while making ceramics. When we cultivate moments of bliss in our lives, even busy times can feel less crazed, and be experienced with greater ease.

Try this:

Take in a deep breath and let it go. Take in another deep breath, hold it for a moment, then let it go. And as you let it go, just allow yourself to feel supported by your chair. Feel the ease of relaxing into the cushion, with no particular demands on you at this time, just notice what it's like to take a break for a moment. Feel what happens in your body when you read these words: *You can relax and feel at ease, any time you want to.*

If you find yourself easing into it, just go with it and relax, letting these words resonate within you.

If you find yourself resisting it, disdainfully discounting it, listen to your inner monologue—"Oh yeah, relax, take a break, that's easier said than done with my busy schedule"— and welcome that, too. Or maybe there's still an active part of your mind that's wondering, "Now what, is this all there is, what's so special about that?"

There may be a protective part of you that gets stimulated, not wanting to get your hopes up only to have them dashed again. That's fine, let's welcome that concern, even feel some compassion for that longing not to be disappointed.

Allow all that chatter to be here, too, all is welcome here, and just watch it as it plays itself out, and come back to this moment, relaxing in your seat, and feel the physical sensations you are experiencing right now.

Proven Ways to Raise Your Set-Point of Happiness

As mentioned in the Introduction, we tend to have a "set-point" of happiness. But only about fifty percent of our set-point appears to be genetic, so there's a lot of room to enhance our experience of well-being in the world.

Martin Seligman's website offers various assessment tools we can use to gauge our starting point, and then see how we're doing as we go along. You can take the *General Happiness Scale*, the *Satisfaction With Life Scale*, and the *Optimism Test*: www.authentichappiness.org.

Jonathan Haidt, author of *The Happiness Hypothesis*, outlines a five-step approach to boosting your happiness quotient (see www.happinesshypothesis.com/beyond-gethappy.html):

1. Assess your current state.
2. Get the support you need for your mental well-being.
3. Improve your personal connections.
4. Find ways to use your "signature strengths" at work.
5. Get in touch with something beyond yourself.

Marci Shimoff, in *Happy for No Reason*, offers a number of ways to develop happiness by nurturing your body, mind, and soul; developing a sense of purpose; and cultivating your relationships. Being genuinely happy without any particular reason may seem like a paradox. And yet, by cultivating these healthful approaches to our lives, we can develop a lovely sense of well-being for simply *being alive*.

Following is a list of attitudes and action-steps that I've gathered from several research studies. All of these have been shown to enhance our moods, reduce stress, and increase our set-point of happiness. Many of these include both short-term as well as longer-term benefits, so pick a few that appeal to you and give them a try. See how they work for you!

1. Gratitude

Keep a gratitude journal. Don't worry, you don't need to write everyday, or even in whole sentences! Just jot down a few phrases that capture your experience.

For example, make a list of five things that you were grateful for in the previous week. These can be as simple as noticing a beautiful sunset or a blossom on a tree. They can also include your health, your job, your spouse, or your children. Try to vary it from week to week, so you become aware of different aspects of your life that you appreciate.

When you go to bed, instead of focusing on everything that's been left undone, and reviewing everything you have to do tomorrow, reflect on a couple of things you're grateful for as you drift off to sleep.

2. Recognize your strengths

Think of a time when you had a challenge that you overcame: what were the hidden strengths that you were able to bring to bear in order to deal with it?

Here's another idea to reflect on: remember a major disappointment, and then what happened afterwards: how did you handle it? Since you didn't get the job, the school, the prize, or the loved one you hoped for, how did your life evolve, instead?

Take the free Character Strengths Test: https://www.viacharacter.org/survey/account/register.

This guide can help you recognize (and appreciate!) some of your own strengths: what you're good at, and what you already enjoy doing. This test will rank your strengths so you can identify the top five. Each day, try to find some way to use at least one or more of your signature strengths at work, with friends and family, or on your own.

3. Appreciation

Share your appreciation for someone important to you. This could be a mentor, or family member, a close friend, or even a former teacher, youth leader, minister, or coach: someone who's made a big impact on your life, who may not even be aware of what a significant gift they gave you. It's helpful to write it down, and share it with them. If they're still alive, and you can actually visit them in person and read it to them, it can be an amazingly touching and powerful experience. Even if they're no longer alive or easily available, just the act of writing it down can also be very affirming.

4. Generosity

Find some way to contribute to others: through "random acts of kindness" during the day, and even more consistently by volunteering or participating in a cause that you believe in.

5. Good friends and family connections

In the midst of our busy lives, it's helpful to make a point of getting together with friends and family members. One of the greatest gifts we can give each other is our loving presence, witnessing and participating in each other's lives. Something as simple as sharing a meal enhances connection, trust, and emotional intimacy.

A wonderful present for a loved one can be a collection of fond memories. Gather photos, and record or write down incidents from a number of people who are close to the one being celebrated. Put it together in a memory notebook, or copy your recordings to a CD or DVD.

I once worked in a clinic where a retreat facilitator asked us to write down a few simple appreciations for each of the people we worked with. Even if we didn't know some of our co-workers very well, most of us came up with a few simple things to say. It can be surprising and delightful to hear what gifts others see in you—and what you appreciate in others, as well.

6. Make something

It can be very satisfying to create something that never existed before. Even if you don't believe you're especially "talented" or "creative," it doesn't matter! It can be something as simple as digging in the garden, cooking a meal, repairing a fence, or decorating a birthday cake.

Having instant access to art, music, and literature from all over the world in some ways inhibits our own natural expression, because we assume we have to be really talented or amazingly creative to express ourselves artistically. Paint, sing, dance, or play a musical instrument for the sheer joy of the pleasure it gives you!

7. Exercise

In addition to helping us stay healthy, regular exercise eases bouts of depression, reduces stress, and helps us feel more alive. Exercise stimulates our endorphins, so we get a momentary rush, or natural "high." Regular exercise also provides a boost in energy that helps regulate our metabolism. We feel fit, healthier, and more capable of confronting physical challenges. Exercise also seems to be beneficial in terms of managing pain. (If you haven't already been exercising, it's always wise to consult your physician before embarking on a new exercise routine.)

8. Eat well

Eat well by noticing your own natural hunger, as well as when you're satisfied. Slow down, really savor the tastes, textures, fragrances, and pleasurable sensations. Take a moment to be mindful of lifting your fork, placing the food in your mouth, chewing, tasting, and swallowing.

Eating mindfully can help with over-eating, because when you slow down enough to enjoy the pleasure of a meal, you're more likely to notice when you're feeling satisfied, rather than stuffing yourself.

Saying grace at mealtimes can provide a mindful pause in our otherwise hectic day. It's a simple way to acknowledge our gratitude for the bounty we are about to share. For those who are not especially religious, take in a deep breath, and appreciate all the people who grow our food, harvest it, bring it to market, sell it, and prepare it for us.

9. Get plenty of sleep!

As a nation, we are sleep-deprived: we get far less sleep than we did thirty years ago. Sleep deprivation is as dangerous as drunk driving, and is the apparent cause of many accidents. So get plenty of sleep! At least seven or eight hours a night. A twenty-minute nap in the middle of the day can also be a great stress-reducer and a wonderful respite from our busy lives.

10. Humor and laughter
When you can laugh at yourself, there is enlightenment.
—Shunryu Suzuki

Developing your sense of humor, and the ability to laugh at your own foibles, can go a long way toward keeping a good perspective on things.

Laughter clubs encourage people to laugh on purpose, for no reason. It appears that the physiological benefits of laughter still kick in, even if we're not initially amused; and a group of people laughing themselves silly can sometimes seem pretty funny, after all!

Even if doing something like that feels too contrived for your taste, it's nonetheless helpful to look for moments of joy, surprise, humor, and wonder. I learned from my mom that it always feels good to indulge in at least a good giggle once in a while!

11. Forgiveness

Holding on to grudges damages us more than it really affects anyone else.

Yet, as a psychotherapist who has worked with survivors of an incredible amount of abuse, I certainly understand it can be difficult to bring ourselves to truly forgive the perpetrators.

Some people try a leap to forgiveness as a "spiritual bypass" because they think it's more evolved, even if they're not ready. It's helpful to be gentle with ourselves, as well. By forgiving ourselves, we may eventually develop more compassion for the limitations of others.

Nonetheless, letting go of everyday slights and disappointments can alleviate a lot of aggravation. In some ways, it's also a matter of where we choose to focus our attention: yes, we could get all worked up about what Edith said about us fifteen years ago, or feel miffed at a friend for not returning a phone call; but we can also keep some perspective by not taking things so personally, and shifting our attention to what's important in our lives, which can help us transcend inevitable disappointments.

12. Get support

Support groups, self-help, psychotherapy, twelve-step programs, coaching and mentoring, massage, exercise classes, human potential workshops, and retreats can all be lovely ways to get support on our journeys.

Simply finding other like-minded people who share your goals can also form a wonderful circle of support, especially during difficult times, but also during times of celebration, acknowledging your achievements, and special occasions.

My mom was part of a group they called the "birthday girls"—women she went to college with—and they got together several times a year for lunch, laughter, and teasing each other about old times for over fifty years!

I started a support group for myself that's been meeting now for over twenty-five years, and it's been a wonderful way to connect with our various perspectives, memories, losses, and triumphs over time. I've been part of peer consultation and mindfulness practice groups, which include collegial sharing, and wonderful feedback about our work. And I also tap into the vast network of personal growth and meditation retreats in the bay area, which is a source of inspiration and practice.

Aside from family and friends, look at your own networks for generating this ongoing support: church, social clubs, sports, school, political interests, and even your own neighborhood.

13. Spirituality, purpose, or meaning

Regardless of whether or not you subscribe to any particular spiritual, religious, or philosophical beliefs, having a sense of meaning and purpose can provide a helpful way to understand and handle major setbacks and disappointments.

14. Mindfulness

Mindfulness has been shown to activate the left prefrontal cortex in your brain, which is associated with increased optimism. It also enhances moment-to-moment awareness, and appreciation for the gift of simply *being*.

All of these activities can help you reduce stress become more aware of your strengths and what you're grateful for. You can also try shifting your mood whenever you get caught in the grip of your usual obsession! As you move through the world with increasing equanimity, may your path be graced with the following simple reminder:

Beauty above me
Beauty below me
Beauty behind me
Beauty before me
Beauty all around me
I walk in beauty.

—from a Navajo chant

CHAPTER 8

STEEPED IN GRACE

DWELLING IN AWARENESS

A mostly empty gourd makes a lot of noise when you rattle it, but a full gourd doesn't make a sound.
—Tibetan proverb

Many eastern traditions have a custom of not saying much about your meditation experiences. Just *be* whatever you are experiencing, you don't have to announce it to the world. Your progress (or lack thereof!) will be obvious to everyone around you. The Dalai Lama commonly deflects questions about his spiritual attainment by saying he's a only a simple monk, just beginning to get an idea of how any of this works. I think that makes a lot of sense within a cohesive culture, where teachers and sages are recognized by their enlightened involvement with their own community.

Yet in our extroverted, multi-cultural society, with many different traditions existing side by side, I believe it can be helpful to provide more personal experiences; not to show off, but simply to share what it's been like to grapple with these ideas, ourselves. Teachers I've studied with often use stories from their own lives as a way to bring their insights down to earth, so others can relate to them.

I don't want to present myself as a spiritual "guru" or highly-evolved practitioner; I'm simply a fellow voyager along the path, struggling to catch myself in unproductive patterns as much as anyone. Nonetheless, the following experience was one of the developments in my practice that inspired this book. So I've decided to share it in the modest hope it may be helpful for others, as we venture along our chosen paths!

Pure Awareness

Mindfulness can help us catch ourselves when we get caught in a negative vortex, and that moment of choice can reinforce our ability to shift our moods. As you become less reactive, you'll become more open-hearted. In fact, this shift can evolve beyond momentary relief, to a profound way of experiencing your life, other people, and the world around you.

While meditating one morning several years ago, I became aware of a subtle, yet clear consciousness shining through me. All my stories and history dropped away, and there was a pure awareness of this most exquisite sense of *being*. Because there was nothing like a story or identity attached to it, in some ways it felt totally selfless—there was no "me," no grandiosity or uniqueness—yet at the same time, it felt familiar, a heartfelt homecoming, my own true nature: as if I were dwelling in awareness, itself.

This felt so poignant that tears came to my eyes, and for some months afterwards, whenever I spoke about it with friends, I would well up with an amazingly fresh feeling of wholeness and love, laughing and even weeping at times, without even knowing why.

I suspect now it had something to do with an acute awareness of the paradox at the heart of human existence: we imagine, and often experience ourselves, as separate— and of course, each of us has a separate body and mind—yet there's an essential loving reality that brings us together, if we let it. A feeling of poignancy arises from this experience of coming home to our true selves, like a wanderer returning from exile.

A few months later, while participating in a workshop at Esalen, I sat in the middle of the circle and turned around slowly, gazing into each person's eyes. I sensed the loving connection of all beings, each with their own consciousness, peering out at one another. I looked outside and saw a Monterey cypress framed by the window, which appeared to me as an object of exquisite beauty. I wanted to embrace the entire world.

Over time, this experience of oneness has faded somewhat in terms of its luminosity. And yet I remember other times and places when I've had a similar experience, but just not identified it in any particular way: while hiking in the mountains, making love, gazing at the ocean; or even something as simple as pouring water into a cup, or walking down stairs. There's a feeling of just-rightness in the moment.

I remember once as a young man looking at my hands, and being struck by the miracle of *cell differentiation:* every cell has the same DNA, yet depending where it is in my body, it becomes part of my hand, eye, skin, or heart. There's an intrinsic wisdom in our natural growth.

The Perfectly Ordinary

A wonderful sensation of well-being can be tempting to hold on to. Yet there is also something very plain, matter of fact, just naturally-the-way-things-are about this kind of experience. I think in some ways that's just as well—it really is nothing special, an ordinary event—and that's partly what's so lovely about it: the significance of commonplace reality, the *perfectly ordinary*, which makes it so readily accessible, at any moment.

I've come back to this insight again and again, not by grasping on to the previous experience, but by simply reminding myself of awareness, itself; in fact, we are *all* embodied consciousness. My own body, my whole sense of being-in-the-world, can serve as a vehicle of perception and awareness. When I'm feeling whole in myself, I can look around as though I were a camera of all the senses, drinking in sights, sounds, sensations, tastes and smells. The inherent beauty of the surrounding world, the pattern of a leaf, or the clouds passing by the moon, all generate a deep well of gratitude.

When I'm in touch with this natural responsiveness, each moment becomes fresh, and new—now this, now that—unfolding in a never-ending cascade of sense impressions: being present, again and again.

Of course, the intensity of any given moment doesn't last, and I don't want to hold up my own experience as anything extraordinary, or that I'm someone special for having it. And I'm certainly not able to sustain this way of experiencing life all the time! Yet having had a glimpse of it, I have a better idea of what's possible.

Rather than thinking of it as anything special, this recognition of the *perfectly ordinary* is simply the realization of what *already is*, if we could only cleanse "the doors of perception" so we can clearly perceive the world's infinite beauty, despite the insanity that goes on all around us.

We don't need to subscribe to any particular religious beliefs in order to experience this feeling of awe that is at the heart of all spiritual traditions. It's available to anyone, believer and nonbeliever alike. It's simply a part of human nature, and something we can all have access to, regardless of one's faith. And I suspect this experience of awe is what's really at the core of all our values of love, empathy, and compassion.

Steeped in Grace

Grace is within you; grace is the Self.

—Ramana Maharshi

We can think of this fleeting breakthrough as a moment of grace—but grace is not rare. We are *steeped in grace*, and we don't even realize it. In the workaday world, it's like we're wearing blinders to keep us from being distracted by the miracles that unfold before us in every moment.

Once on a silent retreat in the Santa Cruz mountains, I was eating my lunch outside on the deck overlooking Monterey Bay. For five days, all our meals had been taken in silence, and this quiet contemplation had enabled my mind to relax considerably. Suddenly, a blue jay let out a single squawk, and I couldn't help but laugh. In the peaceful space I was in at the time, its squawk seemed at once like a protest, as well as a rueful recognition of the poignant paradox of our mortal condition.

Some see grace as coming from the outside, while others see it as a dormant resource within, yearning to be awakened. You can't really force it—just like you can't *make* yourself fall asleep (or fall in love!)—but you can cultivate conditions and circumstances that are more likely to invite grace into your life.

Spiritual traditions and sacred rituals can elicit the ineffable: Hindu or Zen chants, a Catholic mass, Sufi dancing, a sweat lodge, vision quest, or a silent Quaker meeting. Art, dance, music, and poetry can also help us transcend our usual limitations. The natural world beckons us with its own grace, its own natural and awe-inspiring blossoming forth. And encounters with animals, children, or loved ones can move us, when we allow our hearts to open. Use whatever traditions, methods, or resources that appeal to you to awaken the grace of each moment.

Try this:

Allow yourself to go inside for a moment, take in a deep breath, then relax and let it go. Sense what it's like to feel totally at one with the present moment—nothing to do, nothing to perform—just *being* in this moment. No need to strive for grace, just experience what's here, right now. Life is living itself through you. You are already dwelling in awareness itself, steeped in grace.

If the doors of perception were cleansed, everything would appear to man is it is: Infinite.
   —William Blake, *Marriage of Heaven and Hell*

CHAPTER 9

GOT IT, LOST IT

WHAT'S HAPPENING RIGHT NOW?

We vacillate between our true nature and our imagined sense of self.

—Adyashanti

A common complaint among people who have an initial experience of shifting their moods (or even spiritual awakening) is that it doesn't last. It's fairly common to feel let down when that lovely glow begins to fade. The delight of really savoring this precious insight can seem so clear and obvious, it seems impossible to imagine that it won't continue. Yet inspiration comes and goes, just like every other kind of experience. So we may be tempted to hold onto it, only to have it elude our grasp, like mist on the wind.

One of the biggest mistakes of beginning meditators is to assume you're doing something wrong if you're not totally blissed out while meditating. I think this derives in part from the 1960s when meditation was popularized by the Beatles grooving on Transcendental Meditation, as an altered state and a "natural high." Our current enthusiasm for mindfulness also contributes to the notion that meditation can cure whatever ails you, with somewhat unrealistic expectations about what's supposed to happen when you meditate.

In Tibetan Buddhism, they refer to the three "boons" of clarity, nonconceptuality, and bliss; yet we are warned against becoming attached to these states. Of course it's wonderful to have moments of clarity and bliss; and yet, these are simply momentary experiences, and one can be led astray by trying to hold on to them.

Joseph Goldstein relates his own cautionary tale of being in a deep meditative place in India, which got interrupted by a necessary trip home. He couldn't wait to get back to India to resume this extraordinary experience. And yet when he got there, he found it very elusive. He said he wasted an inordinate amount of time chasing after that moment of bliss, rather than letting it go, and paying closer attention to what was happening right now.

Rather than seeing moments of grace or awakening as altered states of consciousness, the teacher Adyashanti encourages us to realize that our usual delusions are the real altered states; whereas awakening is simply becoming aware of the intrinsic qualities of our natural mind: "pure consciousness as it actually is."

This chapter challenges the whole notion of grasping, even for spiritual awakening, and looks at the paradox of how much we gain by letting go. Rather than clinging to the past, we can let go of that tension and return to *our own inner resources* in the present moment.

When an amazing experience has passed away, have we really lost anything? It's a mistake to assume that your current ability to be present is based on the past. The only thing you've lost is the previous moment, which is gone in any event. Cling to its memory, and you miss whatever is unfolding right now.

Try this:
Take in a deep breath, hold it for a moment, then relax and let it go. If you feel that something is missing, just notice your sense of loss.

Allow yourself to become aware of what's behind the grasping: who notices? What's left? What's actually happening, right now?

"The one who notices" is your own awareness, itself; and you wouldn't be aware that anything was missing, unless you still had a felt sense of what it was. Which is suddenly here, right now, again; if only we can pay attention to it. Behind the content of all our thoughts and sense impressions, we can always shift back to this abiding awareness.

Impermanence

Let what comes, come; let what goes, go. Find out what remains.

—Ramana Maharshi

We have seen that we are not our thoughts, roles, stories, moods, or even wonderful events, all of which come and go. The compulsive identification with transitory experience and momentary pleasures—even "flow," peak experiences, or mystical union—only leads to suffering.

In truth, everything is impermanent, nothing remains the same. The earth rotates between night and day, the weather changes with the seasons, our jobs will someday end, our families disappear, and our bodies will age, stop functioning very well, and eventually die. The pyramids gradually turn to dust, and even the earth will one day be absorbed into the sun.

On a less cosmic level, our moment-to-moment experience tells us the same thing: we breathe in, then breathe out. Our hearts expand, then contract. We work, get tired, and then rest. We get hungry, then eat. We get thirsty, and drink. We smile when we're glad, laugh when we're amused, and cry when we're sad; yet moments later, we're in a different mood.

Even while building sandcastles, or towers of blocks with my friends' kids, some of the fun and excitement comes from the imminent threat of destruction—being demolished by a wave, or toppled by gravity—a vibrant sense that this, too, shall pass away. What a great reminder to hear kids squeal with delight when the waves swirl over the sandcastle, or the tower of blocks tumbles to the floor, rather than being traumatized by such momentary losses!

Impermanence permeates reality. Although this basic truth can feel somewhat daunting, it can also be very liberating: when we no longer insist that everything has to stay just the way we want it to be, we can pay more attention to what actually *is*.

A deep and heartfelt poignancy can be felt with the preciousness of our limited time on earth, and this realization can help us develop a keen focus on how we really want to be spending our lives.

What are we trying to hold on to? The idea is not to glorify any particular experience—even spiritual awakening—but to realize that *our demand that it continue* is what gets in the way of appreciating each moment as it arrives.

Try this:

Take in a slow, deep breath, and let it go.

Doesn't that feel nice?

Ah yes, here it is again. It's so lovely, I hope it lasts forever. Whoops, now it's gone.

Now, if I want to indulge this feeling of loss, I get to experience my wanting, my grasping, and consequent disappointment, and then chastise myself for losing that lovely realization.

Or, I can just take in another breath, and relax into what's happening right now. Realization, then release. Realization, then *let it go*. Realization with each breath in, let it go with each breath out. As you let go of your breath, you can also let go of the previous realization, which is already in the past. No use holding on to it, desperately trying to recreate it; just shift your attention back to the present.

We can find ourselves either grasping for a previous experience, trying to escape from our current circumstances, or wishing for a different moment in the future. Just feel that grasping, and see what happens next.

What's happening right now?

Pay attention to that awareness that exists even when you're not having a seemingly transcendent experience. Who are you when you're no longer seeking anything?

Catching Ourselves

Even when we suddenly find ourselves distracted by thoughts—here we are, going down that road again, or hopping on a familiar train—there's no need to castigate ourselves. The realization that we've gotten lost is cause for *celebration*, rather than recrimination. That's really what awakening is all about: catching yourself whenever you've gone astray, because now you can gently bring yourself back again!

This is the practice: catching ourselves (or awakening to the present moment) again and again, throughout our lives.

Intermittent realization is a deepening process. Let's be kind to ourselves, bold in our aspirations, but not terribly invested in a particular result—*the journey itself is our destination*—this is it!

It's helpful to bring a gentle intention to our awareness, especially at first, when it all feels so elusive. As we go along, we expand our ability to be more present, simply because we're more and more aware of our own natural preference. It's not a gigantic effort, no super-heroic discipline is needed, to remind ourselves again and again how we'd rather live our lives.

If you love going to the beach, the mountains, the desert, or the jungle; if you enjoy sitting beside a waterfall or watching the river, do you really have to drag yourself there? Perhaps we love going to natural places because they allow us to get in touch with our true nature. Yet we can develop our ability to realize that insight in the midst of any activity.

While washing dishes, is it necessary to feel burdened by daily chores? Just pay attention to the warm sudsy water, the spray, the light, the smell of soap, the clatter of dishes being rinsed and stacked. Why spend so much of our time judging, evaluating, assessing our experience, categorizing it as good or bad, pleasant or unpleasant, with grasping or aversion?

One morning I was reading *Stillness Speaks* by Eckhart Tolle, while riding the subway from San Francisco to the east bay. As you emerge from the transbay tunnel, you rise above ground and pass over the train yards in west Oakland. I used to have a lot of negative opinions about what I saw as a dreary landscape of box-like factories, warehouses, and railroad cars.

On this particular day, I looked up from my book and was suddenly struck by patterns of black, gray, and ashen white, highlighted by the sun hanging low in the winter sky. Gigantic cranes for unloading container ships, which I hadn't noticed before, hovered against the horizon like the skeletons of dinosaurs. I suddenly saw beauty where in the past I had seen only desolation, because of the filter through which I took in the scene below me. Simply *being in the moment*, without any preconceptions, helped me see the world in a profoundly different way.

Over time, it becomes more and more obvious how you'd like to be with yourself, and where you'd like your attention to reside: in the habitual pathways of negative condition-ing, or in the *open-hearted spaciousness of being*, itself? Can we look at each moment with less jaundiced eyes, to see the miraculous beauty that's spread out before us?

Seeing more clearly will also enable us to take better care of ourselves, and respond with compassion to the suffering of others.

There's no need to hold on to any given experience, because there really is no privileged moment that is more significant than any other. When we're awake to our own aliveness, *whatever we're faced with*, each moment is suffi-cient unto itself:

Therefore do not worry about tomorrow,
for tomorrow will take care of itself.
　　　　　　　　　　—Jesus, *Sermon on the Mount*

There is nothing to lose, or anywhere to get to other than here and now. Let each moment reveal itself in its own natural splendor.

Whatever arises, passes away—
Awareness is all that remains.

CHAPTER 10

HEARTFELT WISDOM

YOU ALREADY ARE WHATEVER YOU'RE SEEKING

*When I look inside and see that I am nothing—that's wisdom.
When I look outside and see that I am everything—that's love.
And between these two, my life flows.*

—Nisargadatta

Heart and mind, love and wisdom: these two aspects help balance our lives. Love without wisdom can be sentimental and foolish. Wisdom without love can be aloof, remote, and removed from ordinary life. Just as a bird needs two wings to fly, so the two wings of wisdom and compassion enable our practice to take flight. So we need both: a heartfelt wisdom, that informs us with wise and loving action. The Vipassana teacher Dipa Ma was once asked which practice is more beneficial: mindfulness or loving kindness? She replied, "From my experience, there is no difference. When you are fully loving, aren't you also mindful? When you are mindful, is this not also the essence of love?"

Developing Compassion

If you want others to be happy, practice compassion.
If you want to be happy, practice compassion.

—Dalai Lama

Compassion is emphasized in spiritual traditions throughout the world:

Jesus encouraged us to "Love your neighbor as yourself," and early Christians used the Greek word *agape* to describe this fellow-feeling of mutual regard.

Rabbi Hillel said, "That which is hateful to you, do not do to your fellow. That is the whole *Torah*. The rest is commentary."

Bahá'í founder Bahá'u'lláh wrote: "Ye are the fruits of one tree, and the leaves of one branch. Deal ye one with another with the utmost love and harmony, with friendliness and fellowship."

An Islamic verse says, "Those who act kindly in this world will have kindness."

A Hindu verse reminds us, "Compassion will prove the means to liberation."

A Sufi chant claims "The open heart refuses no part of me, no part of you."

In Buddhism, the *Divine Abodes* are loving kindness, compassion, sympathetic joy, and equanimity.

A Sikh verse says, "Keep your heart content and cherish compassion for all beings; this way alone can your holy vow be fulfilled."

The Jain sage Mahavira said "*Ahimsa* (nonviolence) and kindness to living beings is kindness to oneself."

Zoroaster said "Love the righteous. Have compassion for the distressed."

A verse from the *Tao Te Ching* says, "The laughter in your eyes lights up mine. I can see my face in yours. Can you see your face in mine?"

The *Seven Sacred Prayers* of Native Americans calls on the Spirit of the South, whose "warm breath of compassion melts the ice that gathers round our hearts" to "dissolve our fears, melt our hatreds, kindle our love into flames of true and living realities."

Ubuntu (from the Bantu) signifies "I am what I am because of who we all are."

And humanists see compassion as a human virtue that we all have in common, which is why we value it in every culture. The philosopher Schopenhauer recognized that "Compassion is the basis of all morality."

Loving presence is the ability to be present in a loving and empathic way: not demanding anything from the other person, just being present. Compassion is not limited to others; we can also develop more compassion for ourselves:

You can search the entire universe and not find a single being more worthy of loving kindness than yourself.

—Buddha

Try this:

Take in a deep breath, and let it go. Imagine climbing to the top of a mountain, where you find yourself in the presence of an all-loving being, showering you with loving kindness and compassion. Allow yourself to bask in that warmth, acceptance, and wholeness. In turn, open your heart, directing this loving presence toward loved ones in your life, toward strangers, and even those who have harmed you, resting in ease, serenity, and joy.

Wisdom

The truest greatness lies in being kind,
The truest wisdom in a happy mind.

—Ella Wheeler Wilcox

Wisdom is not so much about how smart you are, knowing lots of facts, or having vast stores of knowledge. Wisdom is the ability to see into the nature of reality, itself. We begin to see more clearly when we're not overly identified with our thoughts, roles, and stories. We also begin to develop our ability to catch ourselves when we get caught by negative moods, and shift to this wiser, more loving place.

It's not only how we deal with external circumstances that enhances our well-being in the world, but the realization that no matter what happens to us, we are fundamentally all right. And we can trust in our own responsiveness to deal effectively with whatever life brings our way.

It is in this sense that "you already are whatever you're seeking," and nothing can ever take this away from you: that basic experience of "being all right in the world," which is at the heart of this approach.

We have all been conditioned in one way or another through our families, our culture, and through the particular circumstances of our lives. You are naturally influenced by your personality, body type, sexuality, age, and experiences; tempered by values and aspirations, colored by talents, tendencies, and preferences; all of which make up the sum total of this particular you! And yet this exquisite moment-to-moment awareness of *being* can transcend all our stories about this apparent identity.

Mindfulness can help us tap into the essence of who we are, our original nature, the natural responsiveness of a finely-tuned organism, beyond whatever conditioning we may have had.

Try this:
Take in a deep breath and let it go. Take in another deep breath and hold it for a moment, then let it go. What are you aware of now? The awareness that exists behind whatever you're experiencing right now: this is the *source of pure consciousness*, which you have in common with everyone.

Developing our awareness helps make it less likely we'll be slaves to inward grasping or outward stimulation, gratifying every impulsive craving. We can also engage the responsiveness and choice that emerges from our preferences, values, compassion, and wisdom.

As we develop more compassion toward ourselves and others, we may get in touch with heart-felt reactions to the adversity we see around us: poverty, war, and environmental degradation. It makes sense to assert our responsiveness by engaging with the culture: by caring for the well-being of those who are suffering, and by advocating for justice. Rather than perpetuating the very discord we seek to alleviate, we can expand our capacity to engage others with mindfulness and compassion.

Starting out, it's helpful to expend a certain amount of effort, just to get ourselves to sit still for a moment. But over time, we are drawn more and more to that stillness. And by stillness, I don't mean just letting the world go by. I mean a stillness inside, even when you are totally engaged with the world around you.

Try this:

Take in a deep breath, and let it go. Imagine yourself engaged with various tasks: at work, shopping, driving through traffic, washing the dishes. With each task, see yourself as if you were still and quiet inside, mindfully engaged with whatever you're doing, tuned into your underlying wholeness even while you're at work, picking up your kids, flying a kite, or making love.

The Golden Shadow

Whatever you're seeking may be a projection of your Golden Shadow. You may have already heard of Carl Jung's concept of the shadow, which includes those disowned parts of ourselves that we tend to project onto other people: racism, sexism, and homophobia are common examples of the negative shadow. We see traits in the *other* that we prefer not to see in ourselves.

But we can also project positive aspects of ourselves onto others! This is our Golden Shadow: those attributes of others that we admire, which may be clues to our own, perhaps undeveloped, qualities. Yet the fact that we resonate on some level with these virtues, suggests that we, too, have at least the seed of those traits in ourselves, as well.

Try this:

Take in a deep breath, and let it go. Form an image in your mind of someone you admire: it may be someone you know personally, such as a relative, teacher, or friend; or it may be some historical figure whose contributions or qualities you admire.

Name some of the positive characteristics you see in that person.

Now realize that *each one of these strong points exists in you,* which allows you to recognize them in others. They may be in a fairly embryonic stage, but that's all right! Just allow those qualities to sink in, resonating in your heart. Allow yourself to feel, accept, and realize these virtues in yourself, not in some grandiose way, but as a lovely and soothing recognition of your own capacity for fulfillment in the present moment.

Our golden shadow is activated not only by traits in other people; we can also see these precious parts of ourselves in our longing for wholeness. The spiritual quest, the search for meaning, whatever impulse moved you to read this book, reflects a capacity already within you.

You already are that moment-to-moment awareness.

Try this:
Take in another deep breath, and come back to the present moment. What's happening now? And now? Ease into it, allow whatever arises, welcome each moment, and let it go.

You Already Are Whatever You're Seeking

In a way, the very concept of *seeking* is a misleading term, since it implies the experience of self-realization is out there somewhere, and we have to go after it; as if it were a goal to be attained only after many decades (or lifetimes!) of strenuous effort and training. While it's helpful to remind ourselves to be mindful, an arduous striving is the antithesis of being in the present moment. By ceasing the chase, you are already here: awareness is within you, moment-to-moment, and it touches everything around you.

What you expect has already come, but you do not recognize it.

—Jesus, *Gospel of Thomas*

Try this:
Take in another deep breath, and let it go. Allow yourself to get in touch with the full force of your desire for wholeness. This can be a simple, pure expression of being. If there's any tension associated with it, just feel into that tension, crank it up, hold your breath, then let it go. As you let it go, just allow yourself to shift into your own love and wisdom.

Look at you, you madman!
Screaming you are thirsty
And dying in a desert,
When all around you
There is nothing but water.

—Kabir

Whenever you've "lost it," you can always re-enter this precious realization, as though returning home, once again. A perfect, restful state of alert awareness and presence.

As your stories of who you think you are drop away, you discover that *you are dwelling in awareness itself:* you are Christ-consciousness, you are a realized Buddha, you are Brahman, Atman, Quan Yin, Mary, the Tao, nature, or the

Great Spirit—*Tat Tvam Asi*, Thou art That—*and so is everyone else.*

All the various "names of God" can be understood as metaphors or expressions of consciousness, wholeness, and being. They come from many different traditions, and serve as an approximation of that ineffable quality, "a finger pointing toward the moon," humanity's various attempts at expressing the essence of what you actually are.

Ah yes, *this* is who I am, in this moment. I am that wholeness, stillness, or even a fireball of energy. This is home, the unconditioned, the inner sanctuary, the freedom to be as I am. At the same time, to see clearly that separation is an illusion: we are all connected in a vast web of life and buzzing energetic motion. I can learn to trust in my own responsiveness, through a compassionate acknowledgment of others.

You are that source of Love. You are the source of Wisdom. *You already are whatever you're seeking!*

This is our birthright. Even when we're not feeling particularly calm—when we're tossed about like a dingy on a wind-swept sea—we can always come back here, to this calm and mindful place, to tap into it.

You already are Love, Wisdom, and Awareness. All you have to do is notice: just this.

Once you set foot upon this path,
you will see it everywhere!

—Hermes Trismegistus

APPENDIX: GUIDED MINDFULNESS

Practicing mindfulness can help you catch yourself when you get hijacked by your moods. Over time, you'll increase your ability to sidestep negative trains of thought in the first place. Or if you get caught, mindfulness can also help you recognize what sort of train you're on so you can hop off at the next stop—and avoid the usual train wreck!

Many people find themselves floundering with meditation, so the following suggestions provide some structure to settle your mind. Then you're more likely to be calm enough to witness whatever arises without the familiar reactivity of negative conditioning. This calm witnessing may lead to keen insights about your own thoughts and perceptions, and even about the nature of reality, itself.

This practice has created considerable stability, calm, and clarity in my own life. I do not intend it in any way as some quintessential method, it's simply a sequence that helps me become more centered. You may discover other phrases, prayers, or inspirational quotes that help you "settle your mind." Meditation teachers, from many different traditions, can also offer more specific guidance. Feel free to adapt it to make it as relevant as possible for your own practice!

Establish a Setting and an Intention

I light a candle and ring a bell, with the intention of calming my mind, generating loving kindness, compassion, equanimity, and joy for myself and all beings. Equanimity is a feeling of serenity, contentment, and calm, even in the face of difficult circumstances. Thich Nhat Hanh suggests we can access joy by simply easing ourselves into a slight smile, which often stimulates a genuine experience of warmth and well-being:

Sometimes your joy is the source of your smile, but sometimes your smile can be the source of your joy.
— Thich Nhat Hanh

You might want to include a prayer from your own tradition, spiritual quotes, or read a sacred verse. If you're not especially religious, you may simply want to set your own intention of relaxed calm, happiness, love, well-being, safety, and compassion.

Calming Breaths

This series consists of three sets of ten deep breaths. I find these breaths to be very calming. Even when I'm tempted to "just get on with it," I always feel better when I take a few moments to relax into these slow deep breaths.

You may find it helpful to maintain your attention by breathing in through your nose, then out through your mouth, with your tongue placed against the roof of your mouth, just behind your front teeth. (Breathe slowly and calmly, rather than quickly; otherwise you'll get dizzy from hyperventilating.)

Set one: Take in a deep breath, hold it for a count of ten (or five, if ten is too much), then release.

Do this ten times.

Set two: Take in a deep breath, counting 10 through 6 on the inhalation, then 5 through 1 on the exhalation. For ten breaths.

Set three: Simply take in ten slow, deep breaths.

Insights: Dwelling in Awareness Itself

Breathing naturally, with each breath I remind myself of the following qualities that I've experienced as significant, heart-felt insights:

You are embodied consciousness
A vehicle of perception
A camera of all the senses.
You are spaciousness, luminosity, loving presence, and *Being*.
Dwelling in Awareness itself,
Whatever arises, passes away—
Awareness is all that remains.

Awareness of Whatever Arises

Then I try to simply abide in a calm awareness of whatever arises: a focused, bright attention, without clinging, without distraction, rousing myself from sleepiness, calming my agitation, with loving kindness toward myself, and compassion for others.

All sensation takes place in the present. If you drift off, just bring yourself gently back to the sensation of your natural breath as an anchor to the present moment.

When you're first starting out, it's helpful to meditate for just a few minutes, then you're more likely to want more, rather than simply getting frustrated.

Even if your mind is jumping all around like a monkey, as long as you're aware of it, it's still "working." You can simply catch yourself again and again, bringing your attention gently back to your breath and your current awareness.

Shift Your Mood

If you find yourself obsessing about something and you just can't shake it, remember the four steps of **FIRE** Wisdom to shift your mood:

1. **Feel** how the emotional tension shows up in your body.
2. **Intensify** the physical sensation, and hold your breath for a moment.
3. **Release** the tension
4. **Explore** your preference: whether you'd rather feel uptight, or relaxed?

And now, become aware of your own internal wisdom:
What do you know now, from this more relaxed place, about whatever was bothering you? How would you like to handle the situation you're faced with?

Then return to an open awareness of whatever arises. If the same old obsession keeps coming back, just let it run in the background. You can notice it's there, but each time just bring your attention back to your breath and your current awareness. You can also use a word or phrase as a *mantra*, or calming reminder, of your intention: such as loving kindness, calm abiding, or compassion for yourself and others: may I be safe, happy, healthy, and live with ease. This *mantra* can serve multiple functions: it displaces the obsession, increases mindfulness, and cultivates positive intentions.

Dedication

At the end, I like to offer a dedication of my meditation: May all beings prosper and abide in well-being, happiness, and joy.

As a transition to the rest of my day, I remind myself of the quote at the end of the final chapter:

Once you set foot upon this path,
you will see it everywhere!

—Hermes Trismegistus

I ring the bell to signal the end of this session, and then I try (as much as possible!) to maintain my intention to be mindful while engaged with various activities throughout the day.

ACKNOWLEDGMENTS

SHIFT YOUR MOOD is a synthesis of insights from positive psychology, somatic therapy, neuroscience, and mindfulness. I would like to acknowledge the various teachers, colleagues, and friends who have helped me integrate these influences in both my life and practice.

My approach to psychotherapy grew out of the humanistic psychology of Carl Rogers and Abraham Maslow, who advocated a more humane approach to people seeking help. These strength-based, client-centered approaches have been researched and validated through the emerging field of Positive Psychology. I am grateful to Martin Seligman for providing a list of resources and research on specific actions we can take to raise our "set-point" of happiness.

I've also felt drawn to the practical problem-solving approach of cognitive behavioral therapy (CBT), and I've combined this with Gestalt, Psychosynthesis, and insights from Hakomi, a mindfulness-based approach to somatic therapy, developed by Ron Kurtz over forty years ago.

Hakomi teachers have included Scott Eaton, MFT; Jon Eisman; Rob Fisher, MFT; Jaci Hull, MA; and Manuela Mischke Reeds, MA, MFT. Jon developed an approach to state-shifting called "Re-Creation of the Self," and he inspired us to carefully examine how each of us actually makes this shift. This investigation led to my discovery of the *physical* shift that leads to internal wisdom, which underlies SHIFT YOUR MOOD.

I was introduced to the practice of *Vipassana*, or Insight Meditation, by Joseph Goldstein in 1974. He led our study and practice group during the first summer of the Naropa Institute in Boulder Colorado. I've always been grateful for his early influence on my own mindfulness practice.

I've attended meditation retreats at Spirit Rock, where Ajahn Amaro, James Baraz, Sylvia Boorstein, Howard Cohn, Mark Coleman, Jack Kornfield, Phillip Moffitt, Guy Armstrong, Sally Armstrong, and Gil Fronsdal (to name just a few I've been exposed to), have encouraged us to explore a deepening connection with our own experience.

Jack is one of the founders of Spirit Rock, and I've appreciated his insights regarding the interface between mindfulness and psychotherapy. In his book, *A Path with Heart*, Jack quotes the line from a story by James Joyce I could identify with, which I included in chapter 3.

I first met Alan Wallace (author of *Genuine Happiness*, among other books) when we were students with the University of California's Education Abroad Program at Georg-August University in Goettingen, Germany. He introduced me to Aldous Huxley's *Perennial Philosophy*, which describes the common wisdom underlying the world's spiritual traditions. A few years ago, I ran into him again when he was recruiting participants for his Shamatha Project, which trains people in "calm abiding." I was fortunate enough to join him for a week of this practice. This brief experience of *shamatha* has deepened my appreciation for calm abiding as a stable basis for insight meditation.

Adyashanti, a lay Zen teacher, emphasizes Ramana Maharshi's "direct path" of *Advaita Vedanta*, or nondual realization. His insights regarding the common experience of "I got it, I lost it" influenced my approach to chapter 9. And I've taken a few workshops with Myo Lahey, Fu Schroeder, and Tova Green (through the San Francisco Zen Center) at Green Gulch and Tassajara.

I found Satchidananda's surfing quote in Jon Kabat-Zinn's book, *Wherever You Go, There You Are*, and used this metaphor for riding waves of emotion in chapter 1.

I'd like to thank Rick Hanson, Ph.D. and Rick Mendius, MD (co-authors of *Buddha's Brain*) for permission to use their meditation guides in Chapter 3. Their workshops include comprehensive documentation of the neuroscience underlying contemplative practices.

I'm also grateful to Mariah Fenton Gladis, whose heart-felt Gestalt workshops at Esalen facilitated some of my own breakthroughs in countering previous negative conditioning.

In more recent years, I've been in a Mahamudra practice and study group with Andrew Levine as well as Peter Barth, who developed *A Meditation Guide for Mahamudra* under the guidance of Khenchen Thrangu Rinpoche.

Through the Mindfulness Training Institute, taught by Mark Coleman and Martin Aylward, I became a Certified Mindfulness Teacher, and served as a mentor for mindfulness teachers-in-training during their next U.S. training. Mark and Martin encouraged us to teach from our own grounded practice (as they exemplify in their own instruction), and this was a great teaching, in itself.

During the Advanced Practitioners Program at Spirit Rock, I was very grateful for the wise guidance of John

Martin, who provided personal mentoring and also led our local San Francisco section of the program.

What I've appreciated about all these teachers, beyond any particular technique, is their embodiment of loving presence, which exemplifies their approaches to psychotherapy, mindfulness, growth, and healing.

I am also grateful to friends and colleagues who gave me feedback and suggestions in response to earlier drafts of this book: David Bibus; Lynn Blair-Thomas; Michael D'Arata, NP; Diana Gray, Ph.D.; James Guay, MFT; Mark Hall; Bernard Mayes; Gordon Murray, MFT; Lori Schwanbeck, MFT; Will Scott, MDiv; Alecia Vultaggio; and Paul D. Zak, LCSW.

Gordon and Paul offered a great deal of encouragement during the intense period following the experience I describe in chapter 8 (STEEPED IN GRACE), and I am very grateful for their insights, witnessing, and ongoing feedback.

Lori and James were also part of my consultation group, along with Kathleen Dunbar, MFT. Lori suggested the "train pulling into the station" metaphor I used in chapter 5. I'd like to thank all three for their kind witnessing, allowing me to practice with them as I developed this approach; and also for their wonderful encouragement, which kept me on track with my vision for this project. Both Lori and James served as my co-leader for Embodied Mindfulness workshops at Esalen.

And a special thanks to Libby Roderick for her permission to record a cover of her song, "How Could Anyone," for the video about my mom.

BIBLIOGRAPHY

I've divided this bibliography into the following categories:

1. Mindfulness books that highlight the intersection between meditation and psychological well-being.
2. Positive psychology, documenting the new "science of happiness."
3. Cognitive therapy, which shows the influence of our thoughts on our emotional lives.
4. Neuroscience studies, revealing the influence of meditation on brain function and neuroplasticity.
5. Body-mind (somatic) therapy, which integrates mind and body healing.
6. Trauma resources.
7. Perennial Philosophy books from various traditions that facilitate the awareness of *being*, and the experience of oneness.

Here are a few examples in each category:

1. Mindfulness and Psychology

Happiness Is an Inside Job: Practicing for a Joyful Life, by Sylvia Boorstein.

When Things Fall Apart: Heart Advice for Difficult Times, by Pema Chödrön.

Thoughts Without a Thinker: Psychotherapy from a Buddhist Perspective, by Mark Epstein.

Mindfulness and Psychotherapy, by Christopher K. Gremer.

Wherever You Go, There You Are, by Jon Kabat-Zinn.

A Path with Heart, by Jack Kornfield.

Happiness: A Guide to Developing Life's Most Important Skill, by Matthieu Ricard.

Loving-Kindness: The Revolutionary Art of Happiness, by Sharon Salzberg.

Genuine Happiness, by B. Alan Wallace.

The Psychology of Awakening, by John Wellwood.

The Mindful Way Through Depression, by Mark Williams, John Teasdale, Zindel Segal, and Jon Kabat-Zinn.

These books are all excellent resources for developing mindfulness and emotional balance. They also help western readers understand the psychological benefits of mindful awareness. Although mindfulness has a rich history in contemplative traditions as a vital part of spiritual awakening, the practice of mindfulness doesn't require any particular religious beliefs.

2. Positive Psychology and the Science of Happiness

Happier, by Tal Ben-Shahar.

Flow, by Mihaly Csikszentmihalyi.

Thanks! How the New Science of Gratitude Can Make You Happier, by Robert Emmons.

Stumbling on Happiness, by Daniel Gilbert.

The Happiness Hypothesis, by Jonathan Haidt.

The Science of Happiness: How Our Brains Make Us Happy, and What We Can Do to Get Happier, by Stefan Klein.

Happiness: Lessons from a New Science, by Richard Layard.

The How of Happiness: A Scientific Approach to Getting the Life You Want, by Sonja Lyubomirsky.

Happiness—The Science Behind Your Smile, by Daniel Nettle.

A Primer in Positive Psychology, by Christopher Peterson.

Authentic Happiness, by Martin Seligman.

Happy for No Reason, by Marci Shimoff.

Positive psychology and the science of happiness emphasize our internal strengths, not just our neurotic tendencies. These books counter the common assumption that having more money or pleasure increases happiness. They suggest that meaning and connection are more reliable sources of well-being. They also offer proven methods to help us grow beyond our usual "set-point" of happiness, by using our "signature strengths," and by increasing our altruism, generosity, gratitude, and forgiveness.

3. Cognitive Therapy

Cognitive Therapy of Depression, by Aaron Beck.

The Anxiety and Phobia Workbook, by Edmund J. Bourne.

Feeling Good: The New Mood Therapy, by David D. Burns.

Emotional Intelligence, by Daniel Goleman.

Dialectical Behavior Therapy in Clinical Practice, by Marsha M. Linehan.

Peaceful Mind: Using Mindfulness and Cognitive Behavioral Psychology to Overcome Depression, by John R. McQuaid and Paula E. Carmona.

Cognitive behavioral therapy (CBT) has been recognized as one of the best-researched and most effective forms of psychotherapy. The ability to counter negative thoughts and unrealistic conclusions with a more accurate assessment of our true abilities is very helpful in therapy, and I use it a lot with clients, myself.

Cognitive therapy challenges many of the common distortions that creep into our thinking: over-generalizing, all-or-nothing thinking, taking things personally, perfectionism, ignoring the positive and dwelling on the negative, etc. Combining CBT with mindfulness can help us catch ourselves when we're caught in the grip of negative beliefs and assumptions.

4. Neuroscience

Train Your Mind, Change Your Brain, by Sharon Begley.

Altered Traits: Science Reveals how Meditation Changes Your Mind, Brain, and Body, by Daniel Goleman and Richard J. Davidson

Resilient: How to Grow an Unshakable Core of Calm, Strength, and Happiness, by Rick Hanson.

The Mindful Brain, by Daniel Siegel.

My Stroke of Insight, by Jill Bolte Taylor.

These books document how the brain has considerably more *neuroplasticity*, or ability to change, than had previously been thought. Through the practice of mindfulness, agitation is soothed, and our own natural propensity for optimism has a chance to thrive.

5. Body-Mind (Somatic) Psychotherapy

Body-Mind Psychotherapy, by Susan Aposhyan.

Psychosynthesis, by Roberto Assagioli.

The Feeling of What Happens: Body and Emotion in the Making of Consciousness, by Antonio Demasio.

Experiential Psychotherapy with Couples: A Guide for the Creative Pragmatist, by Rob Fisher.

Focusing, by Eugene T. Gendlin.

Somatic Psychology: Body, Mind and Meaning, by Linda Hartley.

Body-Centered Psychotherapy: The Hakomi Method: The Integrated Use of Mindfulness, Nonviolence and the Body, by Ron Kurtz.

Gestalt Therapy Verbatim, by Fritz Perls.

Gestalt Therapy Integrated, by Erving Polster and Miriam Polster.

Touching Enlightenment: Finding Realization in the Body, by Reginald A. Ray.

Somatic therapy is a mind-body approach to help us get in touch with how emotions manifest in our bodies. These books offer various approaches to integrating body awareness and psychological healing. A lot of my own work has been influenced by Gestalt Therapy, Psychosynthesis, and extensive training in the methods of Hakomi, a mindfulness-based approach to somatic therapy.

6. Trauma Resources

Tales of a Wounded Healer: Creating Exact Moments of Healing, by Mariah Fenton Gladis.

Waking the Tiger: Healing Trauma: The Innate Capacity to Transform Overwhelming Experiences, by Peter Levine.

Trauma and the Body: A Sensorimotor Approach to Psychotherapy, by Pat Ogden, Kekuni Minton, and Claire Pain.

The Body Remembers: The Psychophysiology of Trauma and Trauma Treatment, by Babette Rothschild.

One of the challenges of post-traumatic stress is that our bodies continue to react as if we were still in danger, even though the original source of the trauma may no longer be present.

All four of these books demonstrate how our natural reactions can be utilized to heal from trauma, as well. The basic idea is to allow your body to relax in a mindful awareness of your current safety. Then you're more likely to experience smaller doses of your body's activation without feeling overwhelmed or re-traumatized.

7. Mindfulness and the Perennial Philosophy

Emptiness: A Practical Guide for Meditators, by Guy Armstrong.

The Great Transformation: The Beginning of Our Religious Traditions, by Karen Armstrong.

A Meditation Guide for Mahamudra, by Peter Barth.

The Power of Myth, by Joseph Campbell.

The Sufi Doctrine of Rumi, by William C. Chittick.

Dzogchen, by the Dalai Lama

I Am That, Talks with Sri Nisargadatta, transcribed and edited by Maurice Frydman.

Mindfulness: A Practical Guide to Awakening, by Joseph Goldstein.

The Essential Teachings of Ramana Maharshi, edited by Matthew Greenblatt.

The Perennial Philosophy, by Aldous Huxley.

Clarifying the Natural State, by Dakpo Tashi Namgyal.

Mind at Ease: Self-Liberation through Mahamudra Meditation, by Traleg Kyabgon.

Contemplative Prayer, by Thomas Merton.

Eight Keys to Practicing Mindfulness: Practical Strategies for Emotional Health and Well-Being, by Manuela Mischke-Reeds.

The Gospel According to Jesus: A New Translation and Guide to His Essential Teachings for Believers and Unbelievers, by Stephen Mitchell.

Beyond Belief: The Secret Gospel of Thomas, by Elaine Pagel.

Essentials of Mahamudra: Looking Directly at the Mind, by Khenchen Thrangu Rinpoche

Although these books come from different traditions and describe various paths, they all point toward one's own internal experience as the basis for spiritual realization and awakening.

RIK'S PRACTICE

About the Author

Rik Isensee, LCSW is a licensed psychotherapist who practices in San Francisco. He has extensive training and experience in somatic therapy, Gestalt, cognitive therapy, conflict resolution, and mindfulness. SHIFT YOUR MOOD integrates mindfulness and body awareness with the neuroscience of happiness, drawing on Rik's psychotherapy and coaching practice over the last forty years.

Rik is also a Certified Mindfulness Teacher through the Mindfulness Training Institute, and completed the Advanced Practitioners Program at Spirit Rock.

An Invitation from Rik

This book may be just the beginning of your journey!

It's not always easy to integrate insights from a book all on your own. As you've probably gathered, I'm a great fan of coaching, retreats, and support groups to help people continue with their practice.

I offer mindfulness coaching and mentoring for individuals, workshops, and trainings for businesses and nonprofits, with follow-up coaching by phone and video. You can contact me through my website:

www.MindfulnessCoach.com

I would also love to hear your stories about how SHIFT YOUR MOOD has worked for you—and I'm sure that others will benefit from them as well. You can post your comments on Amazon, social media, or other sites where you purchased this book.

May you be well, even in the midst of life's inevitable challenges, and enjoy your presence in this amazing world!